Take On Listening 2
Listening and Speaking Strategies

Nadia F. Scholnick • Burt Gabler

With photographs by Kim E. Colwell

Take On Listening, Book 2, 1st Edition

 This book is printed on recycled, acid-free paper containing 10% postconsumer waste.

1 2 3 4 5 6 7 8 9 0 CUS 0 9 8 7 6 5 4 3 2 1

ISBN: 0-07-236096-8
ISBN: 0-07-121390-2 (ISE)

Editorial director: *Tina Carver*
Developmental editor: *Jennifer Monaghan*
Creative director: *Michael Kelly*
Cover image: *© Lisa Henderling*
Interior designer: *Michael Warrell*
Printer: *VonHoffmann Graphics, Inc.*
Audio recording: *New York Audio Productions*
Photo credits: *Kim E. Colwell*

The *McGraw·Hill* Companies

Contents

Overview

Take On Listening 2 is the second in a two-text series that was developed for adult English as a Second or Foreign Language (ESL/EFL) students. In addition to providing intensive listening skill training, *Take On Listening 2* offers extensive conversation and speaking practice through the use of a variety of learning techniques.

Central to *Take On Listening 2* is the understanding that teaching listening involves much more than simply supplying students with a listening encounter. Students must take a proactive stance vis-à-vis listening comprehension. To become good listeners, students need to utilize specific listening attack strategies and develop appropriate attitudes towards the listening process. In other words, students must learn how to listen. Like *Take On Listening 1*, *Take On Listening 2* facilitates the acquisition of effective listening skills by creating a language laboratory in the classroom where trial and error and risk taking are encouraged through self-directed techniques that train students to develop an ongoing pattern of prediction, negotiation, and renegotiation. In addition, *Take On Listening 2* introduces two new strategies appropriate for intermediate- to high-intermediate-level students and requires that they take even greater responsibility for negotiating and processing spoken language in somewhat more complex contexts.

LISTENING ATTACK STRATEGIES

Take On Listening 2 focuses on the use of nine specific listening attack strategies. They are:

Using What You Already Know

Scanning for Background Information (New to *Take On Listening 2*)

Scanning for the Main Idea

Scanning for the Important Points

Inferencing (Making Intelligent Guesses)

Scanning for Specific Pieces of Information

Using Context Clues

Using Structure and Intonation Clues

Revising Assumptions (Checking What You Understood) (New to *Take On Listening 2*)

These strategies are presented within a context of realistic and familiar topics. Whereas *Take On Listening 1* concentrated on content relevant to students' day-to-day personal experiences, *Take On Listening 2* focuses on somewhat more academically-oriented subject matter. This does not mean, however, that *Take On Listening 2* deals with content that would be better handled in subject specific courses. The emphasis is still on language skill and academic development and the topics are simply a means to assist students in negotiating and articulating language and ideas. Chapter topics such as geography, interviews, and consumer awareness provide a rich context for practicing listening and speaking strategies and for developing cultural awareness. Extensive lecture and note-taking exercises, training in speech organization and delivery, and field assignments which require students to evaluate and analyze information and statistics are also included. All of the lessons in the text reinforce the need for critical thinking and analysis. Because the emphasis is on language and cultural development rather than on highly complex disciplines, *Take On Listening 2* is well suited to both academic and non-academic settings.

Take On Listening 2 also provides a framework through which increasingly complex information and culturally enriching knowledge are spiraled. Exercises and activities overlap, ensuring that past language encounters are reinforced while at the same time foreshadowing language students will later encounter.

Chapter Format: Chapter One

Chapter One is a tutorial overview of the listening attack strategies integral to *Take On Listening 2*. The nine strategies are introduced, with plenty of opportunity given for discussion and practice. Students are told specifically what they can do to improve their oral/aural skills and are challenged in Chapter One to begin developing a more proactive approach toward listening comprehension. Armed with the tools provided in Chapter One, students are then ready to practice using the nine listening attack strategies in Chapters Two through Eight.

Chapter Format: Chapters Two through Eight

Part One   Pre-Listening

Pre-listening activities anticipate the language that will be heard in the main dialogue as well as the general topic of the chapter. Rather than have information spoon-fed by the instructor, students are divided into small groups and asked to pool information, generate ideas, and clarify any misunderstandings within the framework of a support unit. By the time the listening activity begins, students have already retrieved a great amount of the information they already possess about the topic and will be ready to match their concepts of the issues and attitudes discussed with those of the speaker(s).

Part Two   Main Dialogue

The goals of the five exercise types in Part Two are geared alternately towards extracting small pieces of specific information or towards gleaning general information; they are *never* geared toward total comprehension or recall. To help teach students both how to use the listening attack strategies and to develop a tolerance for unknown language, the main dialogue must be long enough so that students *cannot* possibly understand everything on the first listening. Inform students that they are going to hear a very long dialogue or selection specifically designed so that they won't be able to *get it* on the first listening! Also, inform them, however that, by the time they have completed the exercises in Part Two, they will have acquired a sufficient understanding of the material to make sense of the listening passage.

Exercise 1 begins with the first sampling of the main dialogue. Here, students are asked to form a generalized picture of the theme of the conversation (Scanning for the Main Idea), and to consider basic information related to the wants, needs, and backgrounds of the speakers (Scanning For Background Information). Where are the speakers? What are they talking about? How are they related? How do they sound? This exercise encourages students to create a mental picture of what they are hearing to help them predict how nonlinguistic elements of communication contribute to comprehension.

In Exercise 2, students are asked to begin negotiating, through the assistance of structured questions, the major issues (Scanning for the Important Points) of the dialogue. Discussion of the questions and answers allows students to share information gleaned from the main dialogue as well as to share the strategies they used to reach their conclusions. You should act as facilitator in this process by reinforcing the notion that there are not necessarily right or wrong answers. Rather, encourage *all* answers because they provide the means, via renegotiation, by which listening comprehension is ultimately reached. In other words, you want to get students talking about how they used the strategies, correctly or incorrectly, so they can refine the process and improve their listening.

After arriving at a general understanding of the main dialogue, students are asked, in Exercise 3, to listen to the dialogue one more time, but this time only for discrete pieces of information (Scanning for Specific Pieces of Information). Here students are taught to focus their attention on specific aspects of the dialogue and to learn how to filter out extraneous information.

Exercise 4 helps students refine their understanding of some of the more difficult utterances of the main dialogue (Using Context Clues). Specific words and phrases are highlighted and students are asked to negotiate meaning by using context clues.

Exercise 5 provides closure and ensures that all students are satisfied with their understanding of the materials. The questions in this exercise encourage students to discuss some of the more ambiguous notions that arise in the main dialogue and provide them the opportunity to express their personal feelings and experiences about the topic. After students have worked in groups, you should reconvene the class and compare answers.

Oral Journal Homework Assignment

As in *Take On Listening 1*, *Take On Listening 2* provides a journal assignment dealing with the general topic of each chapter as a way of encouraging students to practice their aural fluency in a non-threatening, self-directed manner. At this level, however, the focus switches to journals that serve as outlines for speech presentations which they later share in class. In addition to providing speaking practice, oral journals will help train students to organize information and will encourage them to look at the topics presented in each chapter in a more analytical fashion. With each new chapter, increasingly more sophisticated aspects associated with public speaking are highlighted. Some of the areas covered include the use of spontaneity, the proper use of notes, effective introductions and conclusions, proper transitions, and a number of other techniques which will help students with their speeches.

The journal assignment should first be assigned as homework, so that the students have adequate time to organize and develop their presentations. The oral journals can be assigned at the beginning of the lesson to reinforce the pre-listening practice, or at any other point in the lesson according to the sequencing needs of the instructor.

Part Three   Expansion

This section of the chapter focuses on topics introduced in the main dialogue. Expansion exercises make use of short readings, maps, diagrams, etc. to give students an opportunity to develop a deeper understanding of the topics through group discovery. Expansion activities also provide students further practice using listening attack strategies in a less controlled manner. In addition to pair and group discussion activities, each section of the expansion contains at least one listening exercise.

Part Four   Focus

Focus begins with an examination of how various discrete points of grammar, syntax, or aspects of the suprasegmentals of English can be exploited to further aid in listening comprehension. This portion of the chapter is not meant to introduce new structures. Rather, students are taught to utilize their pre-existing knowledge of grammar, syntax, stress, pitch, and intonation as an additional tool to decipher unknown language. Students are shown that, despite difficulties with vocabulary, speed of speech, or other perceived impediments to comprehension, a great deal of meaning can be gleaned through exploiting the clues provided by specific points of grammar, syntax, and suprasegmentals.

Part Five   Practice

The practice section of each chapter has five exercises designed to reinforce all of the strategies, techniques, and topics previously encountered.

In Exercise 1, students are asked to choose appropriate responses to questions they hear. In Exercise 2, students are asked to select sentences that are correct based on the meaning of what they hear. In Exercise 3, students hear short dialogues in which information changes during the course of the conversation. Students practice the strategy *Revising Assumptions* by answering questions as they listen. Exercise 4 features several dialogues, each preceded by a question. Students make inferences based on information contained in the dialogues. In Exercise 5, students hear sentences that reflect various vocabulary words and idioms covered in the chapter and are asked to choose either the correct new vocabulary term or a definition of the word they hear. The Practice section of each chapter should be presented in a listening lab format. The exercises are not intended to serve as chapter tests! Like other exercises in the text, the Listening Practice exercises do not all have strict right or wrong answers. Again, it is important that you help students identify the specific strategies they utilized to arrive at their responses.

Part Six   Using It

In the final section of each chapter, a highly de-controlled exercise is presented. Students are asked to work cooperatively on a variety of projects, which are product-oriented. That is, through the use of persuasion, negotiation, and compromise, students learn to synthesize their skills both linguistically and creatively. Typically in this section students will develop role plays for class presentation, complete contact assignments in which they must interact in real settings with native speakers, and/or complete problem solving and conceptual tasks. In all cases, students are responsible for both gathering information and presenting it to their classmates.

Group Work

Take On Listening 2 is structured so that many activities are group oriented. Working in pairs or small groups gives students a more active approach to learning. Cooperative learning also encourages students to take responsibility for their learning experience. The tasks in *Take On Listening 2* require that students compare, contrast and pool their knowledge and relevant experiences to gain necessary information while you, the instructor, function as facilitator.

Icons

Audio icons are placed throughout the text to indicate those portions of each chapter that are presented on tape and CD. Similarly, vocal tabs are placed on the audiotapes and CDs so that you can progress through each lesson easily and efficiently. Note that you will need to rewind the tape for those exercises requiring a second or third playing (for example, exercises in Part Two's Main Dialogue).

General Teaching Hints

Students may request to hear a listening selection more than once. This is perfectly acceptable. Research has shown that repeated contact with a listening sample is conducive to the development of listening comprehension skills. In some cases, students might first read the choices in exercises involving multiple choice answers before hearing the tape. It is important to remember that the exercises in *Take On Listening 2* are not designed to test. Every item should be viewed as an opportunity for further practice and development.

You as the instructor should control the length of pauses between exercise items in the chapters. Pauses have not been scientifically measured on the tapes, but rather present a general guideline. Feel free to stop the tape at your discretion.

Audio Program

Audiotapes and CDs accompany this text. Please contact your college bookstore to order them.

To maximize student involvement with the learning and practice of listening attack strategies, and to ensure that students are not tempted to rely on rote memorization of dialogues, tape scripts are not included in this text. Tape scripts are included in the Instructor's Manual.

Instructor's Manual

The text is accompanied by an Instructor's Manual that contains the tape script and suggested answers and follow-up exercises.

ACKNOWLEDGMENTS

We are lucky indeed to have had Jennifer Monaghan of McGraw-Hill/ Contemporary as the guiding force in the publication of this textbook. A Virgo's Virgo, Jennifer patiently labored over every detail of both *Take On Listening 1* and *Take On Listening 2* and was extremely generous about including us in the entire process. We know our experience was unique, and we thank you for it, Jennifer. You're the best!

We are also indebted to Tina Carver at McGraw-Hill, now godmother of two textbooks!

Paul Barboza produced the audio for both *Take On Listening 1* and *Take On Listening 2*. After hearing his work, we hope you'll agree that Barboza rocks!

Thank you to Kim E. Colwell for her amazing photographic contribution to this textbook. Kimmeo, we couldn't have done it without you; thanks for caring and listening and snapping some of the best darn pics on the planet!

Thanks also to Deborah Craig for time spent leaning over the light box helping make final photo cuts.

Friends and family members graciously served as models for photographs in both *Take On Listening 1* and *Take On Listening 2*. Thanks to Terrance Maloney, Sol and Elsa Rael, Michelle Griffin, Jennifer Hammer, and Kathleen Wong for allowing us to include you.

Many thanks to our colleagues and students at City College of San Francisco for their support and encouragement.

We extend our love and gratitude to our families and friends. You inspire us.

Finally, love and thanks to Jennifer Hammer and Bob Leydorf for taking this journey with us. We couldn't have done it without you.

Nadia F. Scholnick
Burt Gabler

Listen In

PART ONE

LEARNING NEW STRATEGIES

strategy
A focused plan of action

In this book, you will learn about listening attack **strategies** that will help improve your listening comprehension and speaking ability. The strategies you will learn and practice are very similar to many of the skills you already know from studying how to read and write in English. Before we discuss the listening skills, let's review the reading and writing strategies that you have already practiced. We can then see how the listening attack strategies presented in this book are similar.

EXERCISE 1

Directions: In small groups, look at the two lists below. Match each skill on the right with its definition on the left.

a) Brainstorming

b) Pre-reading

c) Using context clues

d) Using punctuation

e) Scanning

f) Inferencing

g) Revising

h) Skimming

i) Using grammar cues

j) Thinking about personalities of the people, the setting, and the time

1. ____ Changing your thoughts and opinions about ideas during the reading and writing process.

2. ____ Using your knowledge of English language structure to help you understand more when reading and more clearly explain your ideas in writing.

3. ____ Reading just to get specific pieces of information.

4. ____ Thinking about the people, the place, the time, and so on to help you better understand what you are reading.

5. ____ Thinking about what you know about a topic before reading something on that subject.

6. ____ Reading something quickly to get the main idea.

7. ____ Making intelligent guesses about difficult words/phrases/ideas.

8. ____ Figuring out the meaning of new words/phrases from the sentences/paragraphs they are in.

9. ____ Understanding/expressing emotion and other kinds of meaning beyond the words.

10. ____ Before you begin writing, you think about everything you know about the topic.

Now, discuss how you have used these skills and why they are important.

When you worked in groups in Exercise 1, you probably discussed how reading and writing are much more than just looking at or writing single words. Reading and writing involve the use of many different skills for true communication. Listening is also complex. It's more than just hearing a string of words. In order to be a successful listener, you need to apply the same sort of strategies you use for reading and writing. We will now introduce the nine listening attack strategies that are the focus of this book. Learning and practicing these skills will help make you a better listener and speaker. The nine listening attack strategies are:

1. Using What You Already Know
2. Scanning for Background Information
3. Scanning for the Main Idea
4. Scanning for the Important Points
5. Inferencing (Making Intelligent Guesses)
6. Scanning for Specific Pieces of Information
7. Using Context Clues
8. Using Structure and Intonation Clues
9. Revising Assumptions (Checking What You Understood)

Now, take a few minutes to discuss what you think each of these listening attack strategies means. Part Two will give you more information about each strategy and show you how each strategy works.

PART TWO   LISTENING ATTACK STRATEGIES

1. Using What You Already Know

The first listening attack strategy involves thinking about the issues, ideas, or topics that are going to be discussed. Throughout your life, you have learned many things and have had many experiences. This information will help you in your listening comprehension. Just listening to the words (even if you understand everything the speaker is saying) without understanding the topic is not enough. For example, a native speaker may understand all of the words in a lecture about physics, but without some science background, the lecture will be impossible to understand. On the other hand, a foreigner who speaks almost no English can easily walk into an American supermarket and figure out how to buy something. This is because the foreigner has had experiences with markets and understands the topic of food shopping.

Using what you already know is a good listening attack strategy to use in difficult listening situations.

EXERCISE 1

Directions: *With a partner, write a short dialogue between a worker and her boss on a separate piece of paper. The worker is asking her boss for a raise. Remember to include all the things you already know about what might happen in this kind of conversation. Don't worry about spelling.*

EXERCISE 2

Directions: *Now, take turns reading your dialogues to the class. As you listen to each conversation, write down the worker's reasons and the boss's responses in the chart.*

Dialogue	Worker's Reasons	Boss's Reaction
1.		
2.		
3.		
4.		
5.		
6.		
7.		
8.		
9.		
10.		

EXERCISE 3

Directions: *Now, listen to a conversation between a worker and her boss. As you listen, look at your chart from Exercise 2 and circle the reasons and responses that are similar.*

HOW DID YOU GET IT?	How does your life experience help you become a better listener?

2. Scanning for Background Information

To become a better listener, you also need to think about who and where the speakers are. The way the speakers look and sound can help you to understand what they are saying even if you do not understand all of their words. It is helpful to try and guess as much information as you can about the people you are listening to. Listen to the following example.

From the speaker's tone of voice, we can guess that she is very angry. Because her language is formal, we can make a good guess that she probably doesn't know the person she is speaking with very well. Finally, we hear the word *registration*, which tells us that maybe the speaker is at a school, a motor vehicle department, or a similar place.

Thinking about who and where the speakers are, how they sound, and what they might want or need can help your listening comprehension.

EXERCISE

Directions: *Listen to the following speakers, and then circle the words that you feel* might *be true about them.*

1. excited / upset
   formal / informal
   librarian / student / teacher
   school / restaurant / office
   young / middle-aged / old

2. restaurant / department store
   polite / impolite
   young / middle-aged / old
   foreigner / native speaker
   confident / shy

3. department store / bookstore / registration office
   young / middle-aged / old
   annoyed / confused / worried

4. Place: library / hospital / cafeteria / classroom
   Woman: young / middle-aged / old
              high / mid / low level of education
              excited / bored / worried / annoyed
   Man: young / middle-aged / old
              patient / impatient
              high / mid / low level of education
              excited / bored / worried / annoyed

5. Place: student health center / testing office / workplace
   Man: young / middle-aged / old
              student / teacher
              angry / worried / patient
              rich / not rich
   Woman: young / middle-aged / old
              professional / unprofessional
              doctor / teacher / student / receptionist

HOW DID YOU GET IT?

How does thinking about the speakers help you become a better listener?

3. Scanning for the Main Idea

The most important reason people communicate is to share ideas. When you successfully give and receive ideas through listening and speaking, you should feel satisfied and happy. It is possible to communicate ideas without understanding all of the details. When you are listening to speech in your native language, you can not always hear or understand every word that is spoken. But, you usually have no problem getting the main idea. When listening to English, it is important to concentrate on getting the main idea and learning not to worry about the words or phrases you might miss.

EXERCISE

Directions: Listen to the following conversation to find the main idea. What event are the two people talking about? In the blank spaces, write down the main idea and any words that help you.

Main Idea: _____

Key Words:

_____   _____   _____

_____   _____   _____

HOW DID YOU GET IT?

How does scanning for the main idea help you become a better listener?

4. Scanning for the Important Points

Once you understand the main idea of something you hear, you also need to try to understand all the small ideas or points being discussed. Scanning for the important points is a listening attack strategy that helps you identify the smaller points of a conversation. For example, if you are listening to a news report about a visit to India, the main idea is *India*. The reporter might talk about geography, food, customs, or languages. Each of these important points will usually have examples, and the information will be repeated in different ways.

Good listeners use a scanning strategy to break down and organize the information they hear.

EXERCISE

Directions: *Listen to the speaker. When you hear the bell, circle the important point.*

1. The important point is:
    a) The reporter is nervous.
    b) The prison is very big.

2. The important point is
    a) The women are very unhappy.
    b) The prison is uncomfortable.

3. The important point is:
    a) The cafeteria looks crowded and uncomfortable.
    b) The food served in the cafeteria is poor.

HOW DID YOU GET IT?	How does scanning for the important points help you become a better listener?

5. Inferencing (Making Intelligent Guesses)

The words that a speaker uses sometimes have a different meaning, depending on the situation, the way the words are spoken, the relationship of the speakers, and many other things. Good listeners know that they often have to make intelligent guesses to understand the *real* meaning of the words they hear. This listening attack strategy is called Inferencing. Here are some examples of situations where Inferencing is needed to get the real meaning:

You ask a classmate you have recently met to lend you her brand-new car so you can take a two-week trip. When you ask, she looks at you with a strange smile and says nothing. What does this mean?

Even though your classmate says nothing, you were able to get a strong message: No! You were able to use Inferencing to figure out that, by not saying anything, your classmate was really saying no. Here's another example:

You are at work. You are eating your lunch at your desk. Your coworker comes in to see you and says, *I'm so hungry! Wow, those cookies look really delicious!* What does this mean?

Your coworker was asking you to share your cookies without saying, *May I have some cookies?* You were able to use Inferencing to figure out what your coworker was really asking.

Directions: *Listen to the following conversation. Then, read the statements and decide if each one is True or False. Finally, discuss with your teacher how you used Inferencing to decide.*

1. Don remembers who Kathy is.	True	False
2. Don is good at science.	True	False
3. Kathy wants to see Don's class notes.	True	False
4. Don doesn't want to end the phone conversation.	True	False
5. Kathy wants to ask Don out on Saturday night.	True	False
6. Don wants to go out with Kathy on Saturday night.	True	False

---

HOW DID YOU GET IT?

How does using Inferencing help you become a better listener?

---

6. Scanning for Specific Pieces of Information

Pretend that you are at the airport. You are leaving on flight number 84 from Gate Number 77. The flight leaves at 1:20 P.M. You are waiting to hear the announcement for your flight to begin boarding. The loudspeaker is playing many different types of announcements, including flight times, delays, cancellations, gate changes, and individual messages for passengers. You are listening only for your flight information. Is it necessary for you to listen carefully to every announcement coming over the loudspeaker? If you tried to do that, you would get confused and frustrated. Many times, it is necessary to listen only for specific pieces of information (times, dates, names, places, and so on) without paying attention to everything you hear. You have to learn to ignore the unimportant information and only scan and organize the specific pieces of information that you need. This is an important listening attack strategy.

EXERCISE

Directions: *Listen to the recorded message, and fill in the chart on the following page with the specific pieces of information that you need. Don't worry about spelling.*

	Service	Location	Days	Time	Cost
1.	Prenatal Screening				
2.		Johnson Square Medical Center			
3.		Whitehall ——— ———			
4.				7:00 A.M.– 9:00 A.M.	
5.		Hilltop Shopping Center			
			July 12th– July 14th		
		Metropolitan Cineplex			
				8:00 A.M.– 5:00 P.M.	
6.			Mon., Wed., Sat.		Free
				1:00 P.M.– 4:00 P.M.	
				By appointment	

HOW DID YOU GET IT?	How does scanning for specific pieces of information help you become a better listener?

7. Using Context Clues

Read the following sentence:

Mary was so fatigued that she fell asleep in class.

You probably have never seen the word *fatigued* before, but you could easily guess that it means tired. How did you figure that out? You were able to understand *fatigued* because the rest of the words in the sentence defined the new word for you. The context *she fell asleep in class* told you that the word *fatigued* means tired. Using context clues is a good strategy for both reading and listening.

Listen to the following example. You will hear the word *dehydrated*. You probably don't know what this word means. Listen to the word and the context and try to guess the meaning of the word *dehydrated*.

What does *dehydrated* mean? Circle the correct answer.

a) The plant was yellow and had a new flower.
b) The plant was dry and dying.

You were able to figure out the answer from the context. The words *Tom forgot to water it for three weeks* tell you that the plant was dry and dying. Using context clues helps you understand new words and phrases and is an important listening attack strategy to practice and use.

EXERCISE

Directions: You will hear five short selections. Each selection will contain a sentence with words and idioms you may not know. After you hear the sentence a second time, circle the answer with the same meaning.

1. *a)* She doesn't have enough money to buy meat.
    b) She doesn't have enough money for her needs.
2. *a)* She was afraid.
    b) She was excited.
3. *a)* something that is very clean
    b) something that is too strong
4. *a)* a scientific problem
    b) a scientific idea
5. *a)* a strong and dangerous animal
    b) a new and unfamiliar animal

HOW DID YOU GET IT?	How does using context clues help you become a better listener?

8. Using Structure and Intonation Clues

When you are learning a new language, you often think that structure (grammar and word order) can only help you with your writing and speaking and that intonation (the music of the speaker's voice) can only help you with pronunciation. This, however, is not true. Good readers know that structure gives a lot of information about difficult reading passages. Similarly, good listeners know that structure and intonation often provide very helpful clues to meaning. In this book, you will study how to make use of structure and intonation clues to help you to develop better listening comprehension.

Section 1 Structure

Grammar and word order are not just the rules that you must follow when you use a specific language. Grammar and word order also provide a lot of meaning. When you read a difficult passage, you can guess difficult meanings through vocabulary clues and also use the context that the structure of the sentence provides to understand meaning.

For example, look at the following sentence:

We must reduce our overconsumption of paper or we'll soon be left with very few trees.

You can easily guess the meaning of this sentence in two ways: first from the vocabulary in context, and secondly from the use of the word *must*, which is a modal auxiliary (part of English grammar). Not only do you know that trees are in danger, but you also know, thanks to the grammatical clue that *must* provides, that this is a very serious problem and that we have no choice about what to do to fix it.

If you heard the same sentence, the strong modal *must* would still tell you that whatever was being discussed was very important; you would hear that there is no choice.

Take a few minutes to review the following modals with your instructor. They all are related to the idea of *necessity*, but notice that they become weaker as you move down the list.

Modal	Meaning	Example
Must/Have To	Strong necessity, obligation (Listener is told that there is no choice.)	American students **must** attend classes regularly.
Had Better	Very important (Listener is warned to act.)	If you are absent, you **had better** call a classmate for the notes.
Should/Ought To	Strong advice for how someone will benefit. (Listener can choose not to follow advice.)	If you don't understand what the teacher explained in class, you **should** make an appointment to speak with him or her.
Could	One possible suggestion for how someone will benefit. (Listener can choose this suggestion, another one, or none at all.)	If you are having trouble with a class, you **could** go for tutoring. You **could** also speak with your instructor, or you **could** get a friend to help you.

EXERCISE 1

Directions: Listen to the sentences. Choose the meaning of the modal.

1. a) necessity
   b) warning
   c) advice
   d) suggestion

2. a) necessity
   b) warning
   c) advice
   d) suggestion

3. a) necessity
   b) warning
   c) advice
   d) suggestion

4. a) necessity
   b) warning
   c) advice
   d) suggestion

5. a) necessity
   b) warning
   c) advice
   d) suggestion

EXERCISE 2

Directions: Listen to the sentences. Then choose the sentence with the same meaning.

1. a) You can scrutinize the schedule if you want to.
   b) It's absolutely necessary to scrutinize the schedule.

2. a) I advise you to consult with one.
   b) You can consult with one or do several other things, too.

3. a) That's one place you can find it.
   b) You have no choice. It is necessary for you to look for it there.

4. a) I'm warning you to do this or you will be sorry.
   b) You can do this or something else, as well.

5. a) I advise students to analyze the questions.
   b) I warn students to analyze the questions.

Section 2 Intonation

Intonation, the music of the speaker's voice, includes *pitch* (rising and falling of the voice), *stress* (lengthening or shortening a sound, or increasing or decreasing its loudness), and *pauses* (short breaks in the sound of the voice). Changes in intonation can add a lot of information to what the speaker is trying to communicate. In this lesson, we will take a look at how recognizing pauses can help you with your listening comprehension.

Read the following two sentences in your book:

1. I gave a gift to my brother, John.
2. I gave a gift to my brother John.

When you read sentence 1 with the comma, you clearly understand that I am talking to John and telling him about the gift that I bought for my brother. In other words, John is not my brother.

When you read sentence 2, without the comma, you know that the gift was given to my brother whose name is John.

When listening, you do not have the comma to help you understand this difference. Instead, a pause is used in place of the comma to give you the information that you need.

Example   *Directions: Listen to the same sentences spoken:*

1. I gave a gift to my brother, John.
2. I gave a gift to my brother John.

As you can see, when you are listening, pauses in speech can change the meaning of a sentence. A pause can tell you that the speaker is talking *to* someone, not *about* someone.

EXERCISE 1

Directions: Listen to the following sentences. Put commas if you hear an important pause. Leave the sentence as it is if there is no important pause.

1. I gave the math homework to my classmate Tina.
2. I gave the math homework to my classmate Tina.
3. Debbie my next door neighbor is driving me crazy.
4. Debbie my next door neighbor is driving me crazy.
5. Linda my biology lab partner is really smart.
6. Linda my biology lab partner is really smart.
7. Will you please answer Bob?
8. Will you please answer Bob?
9. Are you going to visit Lisa?
10. Are you going to visit Lisa?

EXERCISE 2

Directions: Listen to the same sentences. Then, choose the sentence with the correct meaning.

1. *a)* I am talking about Tina.
   b) I am talking to Tina.

2. *a)* I am talking about Tina.
   b) I am talking to Tina.

3. *a)* I am talking to Debbie.
   b) I am talking about Debbie.

4. a) I am talking to Debbie.
   b) I am talking about Debbie.

5. a) I'm talking about Linda.
   b) I'm talking to Linda.

6. a) I'm talking about Linda.
   b) I'm talking to Linda.

7. a) I'm talking to Bob.
   b) I'm talking to someone else.

8. a) I'm talking to Bob.
   b) I'm talking to someone else.

9. a) I'm talking to Lisa.
   b) I'm talking to someone else.

10. a) I'm talking to Lisa.
    b) I'm talking to someone else.

<table>
<tr><td>

**HOW DID YOU
GET IT?**

</td><td>

How does using structure and intonation clues help you become a better listener?

</td></tr>
</table>

9. Revising Assumptions (Checking What You Understood)

When people have conversations, they are usually thinking while they are talking. Because of this, people change their minds about things they have already said. Sometimes information that is true at the beginning of a conversation is very different by the end of the conversation. To be a good listener, you have to be ready for these changes. You need to practice checking what you understand with changes in the conversation.

EXERCISE

Directions: Listen to the following conversation. Each time you hear the bell, circle the sentence that you think is correct. Discuss each answer with your instructor.

1. a) The man did something illegal.
   b) The man did not do something illegal.

2. a) The man did something illegal.
   b) The man did not do something illegal.

3. a) The man will have to pay more insurance.
   b) The man will not have to pay more insurance.

4. a) The man will not have to pay more insurance.
   b) The man will have to pay more insurance.

5. a) The man will have to pay the fine for the parking ticket.
   b) The man will not have to pay the fine for the parking ticket.

6. *a)* The man will pay the fine.
   b) The man will not pay the fine.
   c) The man might pay the fine.

HOW DID YOU GET IT?	How does revising assumptions help you become a better listener?

Vocabulary Review

In this chapter, you have learned many new vocabulary words. Let's take a moment to review some of the words and phrases you've learned.

EXERCISE

Directions: Listen to the sentences. Choose the correct vocabulary word.

1. *a)* fascinating
   b) stress
   c) ferocious

2. *a)* Inferencing
   b) pitch
   c) overpowering

3. *a)* structure
   b) scanning
   c) make ends meet

4. *a)* strategy
   b) intonation
   c) fatigue

5. *a)* assumption
   b) brainstorming
   c) apprehensive

6. *a)* clue
   b) dehydrated
   c) structure

7. *a)* good time of the day
   b) plan of action
   c) a nice quiet place

8. *a)* memory
   b) statement
   c) guess

9. *a)* reading
   b) changing
   c) brainstorming

10. *a)* cook a big meal
    b) buy enough meat
    c) have enough money

PART THREE

ORAL JOURNAL HOMEWORK ASSIGNMENT

In this book, you will give short speeches about the topics you discuss in each chapter. To prepare for these Oral Journal Homework Assignments you will need to write outlines.

Writing an outline is an excellent way to organize information for a speech. If you create an outline of what you are going to say, it will help you be sure to include all of the important main points and subpoints of your topic. Think of an outline as being like a map. If you are visiting a new place and don't know where things are, a map will help guide you to your destination. Just like a map, an outline will help guide you in organizing information for a speech. The outline will help you be better prepared.

Let's take a look at how to prepare an outline. We will use the topic "What I miss most about my city."

First, you should brainstorm everything that you can think of about the topic. For example, you might come up with the following ideas:

Family	Museums	Shopping
Friendliness of People	Friends	Restaurants
Mountains	Low Crime Rate	Clean Air
Four Seasons	Lakes	Homemade Pecan Pies
The Way People Talk	Big Cheap Steaks	Low Cost of Living
Museum of Agriculture	Annual Labor Day Town Picnic	Good Public Transportation

After you have finished brainstorming, you need to organize your list and see which items logically belong together and delete those that you do not really find very important. For this topic, you could arrange the ideas into the following categories:

People	Environment	Lifestyle
Family	Mountains	Good Public Transportation
Friends	Lakes	Low Cost of Living
	Clean Air	Low Crime Rate

Once you have organized your brainstorming ideas into categories, you are ready to prepare an outline for your report. Your outline will include both main ideas and supporting details. When writing an outline for a speech, you do not have to worry about using perfect grammar or fancy vocabulary. You do not write full sentences in an outline. The outline contains the ideas which will help you remember what to say in your speech. You must be able to speak in your own words and not read your speech. The outline will help you remember what to say.

When making an outline, use traditional numbers and letters to indicate (show) the main points and subpoints. Use Roman numerals for the main points, capital letters for the subpoints, Arabic numbers for the supporting details, and lowercase letters for further supporting details. Here's how the home city information could be organized in an outline:

Topic: What I Miss Most about My City

I. Introduction
II. People
   A. Family (parents)
      1. Getting older
         a. want to see them more often
         b. want to learn more about their history
      2. Worried that they need me to help them more
         a. live very far away
         b. no one nearby to help them
   B. Friends
      1. Feel like we're becoming strangers
      2. Miss talking/sharing thoughts
      3. Feel like a stranger to their children
III. Environment
   A. Mountains
      1. Summer
         a. hiking and camping out
            sleep under the stars
         b. biking
            visit nearby villages
      2. Winter
         a. skiing
            stay in cabin w/friends
   B. Lakes
      1. Summer
         a. swimming
         b. water skiing
      2. Winter
         a. ice skating
            ice sculpture festival
   C. Clean Air
      1. Better for health
IV. Lifestyle
   A. Good public transportation
      1. Fast
      2. Cheap
      3. Convenient hours
   B. Low cost of living
      1. Rent very cheap
      2. Food very cheap
   C. Low crime rate
      1. Streets safe and clean
      2. People can walk late at night
V. Conclusion

Now that you have your main ideas and details, you need to find an interesting way to introduce your speech. Below is an example of how you could introduce the speech about your home city:

Our city is made up of people from all over the world. Like many people here, I come from another place. Although I love my new city, there are still many things I miss about my home town.

Finally, you need to make sure that your audience has clearly understood everything that you have discussed. A good, short conclusion will help the audience feel satisfied that they have learned something important. Here is an example of a conclusion for the speech about your home city:

Of course I am happy living here, but I will always feel that a part of me is still in my home town. While I do get to visit often, I still miss the people, the environment, and the lifestyle that I have left behind.

PART FOUR

USING IT: MY HOME TOWN

Directions: *Use the outline writing technique you studied in Part Three to create a speech on the topic:* What I miss about my home city/country. *Note: If you are living in your home city, change the topic to:* What I like best about this city/country.

After you have finished your outline, write out the full introduction and conclusion for your speech. Then you are ready to practice your speech. Remember the following points for good speeches:

1. Do not read your speech. You may use your outline, but you must know what you are talking about before you get in front of your audience.

2. Maintain eye contact with your audience. Look at them, not at your paper.

3. Speak in a loud, clear voice. Make sure that everyone can hear you.

4. Try not to be nervous or move around too much.

5. Remember to breathe! If you get nervous and need to stop speaking briefly, don't worry about it. Just keep going when you are ready.

6. Try to have fun. Everyone is nervous when giving a speech. Your classmates and instructor will be supportive and help you feel comfortable, so try your best and don't worry if you make a mistake.

CHAPTER TWO

2

Kicking the Habit

PRE-LISTENING: HEALTH SURVEY

genetic
Inherited from your parents

How healthy you are depends on two important things: **genetics** and your own personal lifestyle habits. There is very little you can do about your genetic background, but there is a lot you can do to develop lifestyle habits that improve your health and fitness.

EXERCISE 1

Using What You Already Know

Directions: Take the following survey to find out how healthy your lifestyle is. For each section, read the question, and circle the answer that best describes the way you now live. When you have finished each part, write your total score.

Health Survey

Smoking If you never smoked or are an ex-smoker, enter a total score of 10, and move on to the next section.	Yes	No
1. Do you smoke less than ten cigarettes a day?	1	0
2. Have you cut down on smoking?	1	0
3. Do you plan to quit smoking soon?	1	0
4. Are you trying to quit smoking?	2	0
Total score for this section:		

Alcohol and Drugs	Frequently	Sometimes	(Almost) Never
1. Do you drink more than two drinks a day?	0	1	2
2. Do you use alcohol or other drugs to help you relax?	0	1	2
3. If you drink or use alcohol too much, how often do you try to cut down on your alcohol or drug use? (If you don't drink alcohol or use drugs too much, give yourself **2** points.)	0	1	2
4. Do people tell you that you use alcohol or drugs too much?	0	1	2
5. Do you ever use other people's prescription drugs?	0	1	2
Total score for this section:			

depressed
Very sad

Stress	Frequently	Sometimes	(Almost) Never
1. Do you feel nervous or **depressed**?	0	1	2
2. Can you relax easily?	2	1	0
3. Are you worried about the future?	0	1	2
4. Do you have close friends you can talk to about personal matters?	2	1	0
5. Are you active in any organizations or clubs, or do you have hobbies?	2	1	0
Total score for this section:			

aerobic
Running, swimming, quick walking, bicycling, and so on

Fitness	Frequently	Sometimes	(Almost) Never
1. Do you do **aerobic** exercise for fifteen to twenty minutes at least three times a week?	4	2	0
2. Are you at or near the weight that you should be?	3	1	0
3. Do you have a job or other daily activity that keeps you physically active?	2	1	0
4. Do you do stretching exercises at least three times a week?	1	0	0
Total score for this section:			

cholesterol
Kind of fat found in red meats, eggs, butter, cream, and organ meats such as liver

Nutrition	Frequently	Sometimes	(Almost) Never
1. Do you eat different kinds of food each day (fruits and vegetables; whole grain breads and cereals; lean meats, fish, poultry, and beans; dairy products)?	2	1	0
2. Do you eat a high-fiber diet, lots of whole-grain breads and cereals, fresh fruits, and fresh vegetables?	2	1	0
3. Do you try not to eat foods that have a lot of saturated fat and **cholesterol**?	2	1	0
4. Do you try not to eat salty food or add salt?	2	1	0
5. Do you try not to eat more than three or four sugary snacks, desserts, or soft drinks each week?	2	1	0
Total score for this section:			

Survey Results

How did you do? Go back to each section and find your total score. Write each total score in the spaces below.

Smoking   _____

Alcohol and Drugs   _____

Stress   _____

Fitness   _____

Nutrition   _____

For each lifestyle factor, if your score is:

10–9:   You're taking excellent care of yourself in this area.

8–6:   Your lifestyle is pretty healthy, but take a second look at any questions in this area where you scored a 0 or 1 and think about how you might raise your score.

5–3:   You probably need help changing your lifestyle in this area and need more information to make the correct changes.

2–0:   Your health is probably in serious danger. You need to make some big changes. You need to talk with a health or fitness professional.

Compare your scores in groups. Who has the healthiest lifestyle?

PART TWO

MAIN DIALOGUE

EXERCISE 1

Scanning for the Main Idea/Background Information

Directions: Listen to the dialogue and try to get a general idea of what is happening. Remember, you don't need to understand everything. Just try to think about the following questions:

1. What is the main idea of this dialogue?
2. Where do you think the dialogue is taking place?
3. What is the relationship between the speakers?
4. How old do you think the speakers are?
5. How do you think each speaker sounds (warm, cold, concerned, angry, and so on)?

EXERCISE 2

Scanning for the Important Points

Directions: Now, listen to the dialogue again to answer these questions:

1. What kind of restaurant is the Multiple Organic Diner?
2. Who has been to this restaurant before: Emily, Vicky, or Larry?
3. Vicky is afraid to stop smoking. Why?
4. What does Larry want to order?
5. According to Emily, what two things are important for good health?
6. What are Vicky and Larry going to start doing on Monday?
7. How does Emily want to celebrate their decision?
8. How do Vicky and Larry want to celebrate their decision?

EXERCISE 3

Scanning for Specific Pieces of Information

Directions: Listen to the dialogue one more time. For each item in the chart, put a check (✔) under the name of the person for whom the item is true; put an (x) under the name of the person for whom the item is not true, and put a question mark (?) under the name of the person if you cannot tell whether the item is true.

	Emily	Vicky	Larry
Smokes			
Has already stopped smoking			
Needs to lose weight			
Drinks alcohol			
Loves health food			
Loves red meat			
Loves running			
Loves swimming			
Loves handball			
Loves tennis			
Needs to become healthier			

EXERCISE 4

Vocabulary in Context

Directions: *Listen to the sentences from the dialogue and circle the answer that has the same meaning.*

1. **a)** I think this restaurant might be dirty and uncomfortable.
   b) I think this restaurant might be too expensive.

2. **a)** I thought you wanted to stop smoking.
   b) I thought you wanted to begin exercising.

3. **a)** The food is good for you.
   b) The food is delicious.

4. **a)** Hamburgers make you feel full.
   b) Hamburgers are bad for your health.

5. **a)** I don't want to wear black clothes.
   b) I don't want to become a widow.

6. **a)** It has a chocolate flavor.
   b) It gives you a lot of energy.

EXERCISE 5

Directions: *In pairs or small groups, discuss the following questions. Then, as a class, compare your answers.*

1. How do you think Emily feels at the end of the dialogue?

2. Do you think Larry will quit drinking and Vickie will quit smoking? Why/Why not?

3. Have you ever eaten at a vegetarian restaurant? If yes, describe the meal and what you thought of it.

4. Have you ever been on a diet? If yes, describe the diet, why you were on it, and what the results were.

5. What one thing about your lifestyle would you like to change (for example, would you like to quit smoking, eat better, or exercise more)? Why? What do you plan to do to change it?

Oral Journal Homework Assignment

Directions: *Prepare a short talk about your health and fitness. To help you prepare your speech, use the rough outline below.*

I.   Introduction
     General statements about your health
II. Your Health Habits
     A. Diet
         1. Healthy things you do
            a.
            b.
         2. Unhealthy things you do
            a.
            b.

B. Your fitness
1. Healthy things you do
   a.
   b.
2. Unhealthy things you do
   a.
   b.
C. Smoking/Drugs/Alcohol
   1.
   2.
D. Stress
   1. Stresses in your life
   2. Things you do to reduce stress
III. Future plans
A. Improvements
   1.
   2.
B. Changes
   1.
   2.
IV. Conclusion

In your introduction to this speech, you might want to talk about how important being healthy and fit are. In your conclusion, you might want to talk about any advice you have for your classmates about becoming healthy and fit. You can also include a personal or funny story in your introduction or conclusion to help make your points.

PART THREE

EXPANSION

Section 1 Diet and Exercise
Directions: Read the following passage and discuss it with your instructor.

EXERCISE 1A

obesity
Being very overweight

conscious
To know about or be aware of something

The average American is overweight. There are many reasons for this. One major reason is that many Americans don't get enough exercise. In the United States, machines do most of the kind of work that people in other parts of the world must do themselves. Another cause of **obesity** is that Americans often eat when they are not hungry. People eat when they are happy, when they are sad, or when they are lonely or bored. Because of this problem of obesity, Americans have become very diet **conscious**.

Today, Americans are very interested in diet and exercise. Just go to any bookstore and you will see shelves filled with books about diet and exercise. Look through your TV listings and you will see that there are many shows about these two topics. New diet and exercise programs are introduced each year, but not all of them work and, more important, not all of them are safe. If you are interested in starting a diet or exercise program, you should first consult your doctor.

EXERCISE 1B

Directions: With a partner, study the Suggested Body Weights table to answer the following questions.

1. Is your body weight correct for your height?

2. About how many pounds are included in each range of weights listed in this chart?

3. For a man who is five feet ten inches tall the range is 140 to 174 pounds. Does this mean that any weight between 140 and 174 pounds is good for a five-foot-ten-inch man? If not, why not?

4. The range for a woman who is five feet six inches tall is 114 to 146 pounds. What would be a good weight for a five-foot-six-inch woman who has a large build? (Give a weight with a ten-pound range.) For a five-foot-six-inch woman who has a small build? For a five-foot-six-inch woman who has an average build?

5. What do you think is an acceptable weight range for a five-foot man?

6. What do you think is an acceptable weight range for a six-foot-two-inch woman?

Suggested Body Weights		
Range of Acceptable Weights		
Height (feet-inches)	Men (pounds)	Women (pounds)
4'10"		91–119
4'11"		94–122
5'0"		96–125
5'1"		99–128
5'2"	112–141	102–131
5'3"	115–144	105–134
5'4"	118–148	108–138
5'5"	121–152	111–142
5'6"	124–156	114–146
5'7"	128–161	118–150
5'8"	132–166	122–154
5'9"	136–170	126–158
5'10"	140–174	130–163
5'11"	144–179	134–168
6'0"	148–184	138–173
6'1"	152–189	
6'2"	156–194	
6'3"	160–199	
6'4"	164–204	

Note: Height without shoes; weight without clothes.

Source: HEW conference on obesity.

EXERCISE 1C

Directions: *Look at the Suggested Body Weights table again while you listen to the following questions. Take notes on a separate piece of paper. Then, write the correct answers in the spaces.*

1. _____

2. _____

3. _____

4. _____

5. _____

6. _____

EXERCISE 1D

Directions: *Listen to the following descriptions and fill in the correct information you hear for each person. Then, decide whether each person is at the correct weight.*

	Sex	Build	Height	Weight
1.				
2.				
3.				
4.				
5				
6.				

Section 2 Counting Calories

A calorie is a unit used to measure the amount of energy that each kind of food contains. If you take in more calories than the amount of energy your body uses, you gain weight. If you take in fewer calories than the amount of energy your body uses, you lose weight. One pound of weight equals 3,500 calories.

EXERCISE 2A

Directions: *With a partner, study the Calorie Contents of Selected Foods table on the next two pages to answer the following questions.*

1. Look at the Meats and Poultry section. Which food has the fewest calories? Is this food really the lowest in calories? Why or why not?

2. Look at the Fish and Shellfish section. How big is a portion of cod that has 170 calories? How many calories are in a seven-ounce portion of salmon?

3. How many calories are there in two eggs? How many calories are there if you fry the eggs in two pats of butter? How many calories are there in a breakfast of two fried eggs (fried in two pats of butter), two pieces of white toast with two pats of butter, one cup of orange juice, and one cup of coffee with two teaspoons of sugar?

4. If you were very hungry, but you didn't want to take in a lot of calories, which dessert or snack food would be your best choice?

5. About how many calories are there in a salad made of four cups of lettuce, one cup of cucumbers, two tomatoes, and three tablespoons of French dressing?

EXERCISE 2B

Directions: *Listen to the following questions and take notes. Then, look at the Calorie Contents of Selected Foods table to answer the questions.*

1. _____

2. _____

3. _____

4. _____

5. _____

6. _____

7. _____

8. _____

9. _____

10. _____

Calorie Contents of Selected Foods
(Numbers are rough approximations)

Meats and Poultry

Bacon, 2 slices	95
Chicken*	216
Hamburger*	286
Hot dog*	304
Pork*	373
Steak*	473
Turkey*	263

* = 3 1/2 Ounces

Fish and Shellfish

Cod*	170
Crab*	93
Fish Sticks*	176
Flounder*	79
Salmon*	217
Shrimp* (fried)	225
Tuna* (canned)	197

* = 3 1/2 Ounces

Fruit

1 apple	70
1 banana	130
1 cup fruit cocktail	195
1 cup grapes	102
1 orange	60
1 peach	33
1 cup pineapple	75

Vegetables

6 spears asparagus	20
1 cup broccoli	50
1 cup carrots	20
1/2 cup cucumbers	10
2 cups lettuce	15
1 pickle	11
1 potato (baked)	145
1 tomato	25

Dairy

American cheese*	106
Cottage cheese (1/2 cup)	117
Monterey jack cheese*	106
Swiss cheese*	107
1 egg	79
1 cup whole milk	157
1 cup low-fat yogurt	120

* = 1 Ounce

Desserts and Snacks

1 slice apple pie	330
1 oz. chocolate	151
1 slice chocolate cake	420
1 cookie	110
1 doughnut	135
1/2 cup peanuts	421
1 cup popcorn	23
10 potato chips	114

Grains

1 slice white bread	60
1 slice rye bread	55
1 slice whole wheat bread	55
2 crackers	35
1 cup macaroni	155
1 cup oatmeal	150
1 slice pizza	180
1 cup rice	205
1 roll	160

Miscellaneous Items

1 pat butter	36
1 tbsp. honey	64
1 tbsp. jam	55
1 tbsp. ketchup	19
1 tsp. mustard	4
1 tbsp. peanut butter	93
Salad dressing (1 tbsp.)	
Blue cheese	90
French	60
Mayonnaise	110
Thousand Island	75
1 tsp. sugar	18

Beverages

12 oz. beer	150
1 cup coffee	2
1 oz. liquor	80
1 cup orange juice	120
8 oz. soda	105
1 cup tea	2
3 oz. wine	75

EXERCISE 2C

Directions: *You will hear five customers ordering food in a restaurant. Write each customer's order in the spaces.*

Customer 1

S and G Cafe			
Table	Guests	**71710**	Server
		Tax	
		Total	
Thank You — Please Come Again			

Customer 2

S and G Cafe			
Table	Guests	**71711**	Server
		Tax	
		Total	
Thank You — Please Come Again			

Customer 3

S and G Cafe			
Table	Guests	**71712**	Server
		Tax	
		Total	
Thank You — Please Come Again			

Customer 4

S and G Cafe			
Table	Guests	**71713**	Server
		Tax	
		Total	
Thank You — Please Come Again			

Customer 5

S and G Cafe			
Table	Guests	**71714**	Server
		Tax	
		Total	
Thank You — Please Come Again			

EXERCISE 2D

Directions: *Now figure out the total number of calories for each order in Exercise 2C. In pairs or small groups, compare your answers. Which meal is the healthiest? Why?*

Customer 1   _____

Customer 2   _____

Customer 3   _____

Customer 4   _____

Customer 5   _____

PART FOUR

FOCUS: CONDITIONALS

You have already studied conditional sentences and know that when you hear an *if* clause, the result can happen when and *only* when the condition (in the *if* clause) occurs. In other words, without the action in the *if* clause, the result cannot happen.

Look at the following sentence:

If I have the money, I *will* join a health club.

You know that one thing must happen before I can join the health club: I must have the money. You also know that this is a *real conditional sentence* because the verb *have* in the *if* clause is in the simple present tense. Real conditional sentences tell you that the results are *possible* although they are not certain to happen.

EXERCISE 1

Directions: *Listen to the following real conditional or result clauses and circle the clauses that can be joined to them.*

Example: *a)* I will join the health club.
        b) I will work hard.

1. *a)* if her doctor tells her to.
    b) if she loses weight.

2. *a)* if he loses fifteen more pounds.
    b) if he looks very handsome.

3. *a)* you won't be so lazy.
    b) your fitness will improve.

4. *a)* if she wants to stay healthy.
    b) if she feels healthy.

5. *a)* she will take in too many calories.
    b) chocolate cake will be her favorite dessert.

Now look at this sentence:

If I had the money, I would join the health club.

You know that this is an *unreal conditional sentence* because the verb *had* in the *if* clause is in the simple past. The simple past in the *if* clause tells you that the result cannot happen because the condition does not really exist. The speaker has no reason to believe that the result can or will happen.

Therefore, I will not join the health club because I do not believe that I will have the money. I can only imagine (dream about) joining the health club. Unreal conditional sentences make predictions about events based on imaginary conditions. They are useful because they show how the speaker believes events would or could occur if unreal conditions became real.

EXERCISE 2

Directions: Listen to the following unreal conditional or result clauses and circle the clauses that can be joined to them.

Example: ⓐ I would join the health club.
          b) I would work hard.

1. *a)* her doctor would tell her to.
  b) she would lose weight.

2. *a)* he would lose fifteen more pounds.
  b) he would look very handsome.

3. *a)* if you weren't so lazy.
  b) if you improved your fitness.

4. *a)* she would stay healthy.
  b) she would need a diet.

5. *a)* if she took in too many calories.
  b) if chocolate cake were her favorite.

Review

When you hear a real conditional sentence, which uses the simple present tense, you know that the speaker believes that the result is possible. You do *not* have to understand every word to know that the result is possible.

When you hear an unreal conditional sentence, which uses the simple past tense, you know that the speaker believes that the result is not possible. You do *not* have to understand every word to know that the result is not possible.

Your knowledge of real and unreal conditional sentences will help you be a better listener and understand some very important information.

Directions: Listen to the following sentences. Then, circle the correct answer.

Example: *a)* I might join a health club.
b) I won't join a health club.

1. *a)* I might go running with you.
   b) My knees are not strong.

2. *a)* Eddie will quit smoking.
   b) Eddie's health might improve.

3. *a)* I live near the park.
   b) I won't go running every day.

4. *a)* I might join a health club.
   b) I won't get in shape.

5. *a)* Ling might keep abusing narcotics.
   b) The police won't incarcerate her.

6. *a)* I won't only eat a salad.
   b) I might be famished later.

7. *a)* You might feel calmer.
   b) You won't feel calmer.

8. *a)* I might eat it regularly.
   b) I won't eat it regularly.

9. *a)* We might work out.
   b) We won't lose the battle.

10. *a)* You might stop noshing.
    b) You won't stop noshing.

Remember, you don't need to understand every word to understand whether the speaker believes that the result is possible!

PART FIVE

PRACTICE

EXERCISE 1

Directions: You will hear ten questions. Read the three possible responses and circle the correct answer.

1. *a)* I will go on a diet and exercise more.
   b) I'm not sure. I need to talk to my doctor about that.
   c) Yes, I want to lose some weight.

2. *a)* Cheese is delicious.
   b) It's low in calories and high in fiber.
   c) It will lower your cholesterol.

3. *a)* a hamburger
   b) an apple
   c) a glass of milk

4. a) No, I should.
   b) Yes, I should.
   c) Yes, I shouldn't.

5. a) I have been jogging for about six months.
   b) Every Monday, Wednesday, and Friday and every other Sunday.
   c) I already look and feel much better.

6. a) It's high in cholesterol.
   b) It's high in fat.
   c) It's high in vitamins.

7. a) A calorie is used to measure energy.
   b) Steak has more calories than chicken.
   c) I don't remember. Let's check the book.

8. a) No, my sister is short.
   b) She's tall with an average build.
   c) My sister loves dairy products.

9. a) After I talk to my doctor.
   b) When I lose weight.
   c) I want to lose fifteen pounds.

10. a) He smokes and drinks too much.
    b) He has a really large build.
    c) He should try jogging.

EXERCISE 2

Directions: You will hear ten sentences. Read the three choices and circle the correct answer.

1. a) I hope you will play tennis with us.
   b) I know you won't play tennis with us.
   c) I think you can play tennis with us.

2. a) A plain hot dog has more calories.
   b) A turkey sandwich with mayonnaise has more calories.
   c) A hot dog is more nutritious.

3. a) I like my weight.
   b) I want to lose more weight.
   c) I have lost fifteen pounds.

4. a) I am going to go swimming every day.
   b) I might go swimming every day.
   c) I'm not going to go swimming every day.

5. a) Goldsmith's is open Saturday night.
   b) Goldsmith's is open Wednesday night.
   c) Goldsmith's is open Monday afternoon.

6. a) Frances smokes and hates to exercise.
   b) Dan smokes and hates to exercise.
   c) They both smoke and hate to exercise.

7. **a)** She's probably eating well and exercising regularly.
   b) Her health is probably in serious danger.
   c) She probably needs help changing her lifestyle.

8. **a)** Americans have become obese in the last few years.
   b) Americans have recently become interested in diet and exercise.
   c) Americans eat when they aren't hungry and don't get exercise enough.

9. **a)** You work at a restaurant.
   b) You need to watch your weight.
   c) Your weight is not a problem.

10. **a)** He probably has many hobbies.
    b) He probably exercises three times a week.
    c) He probably has trouble relaxing.

EXERCISE 3

Directions: *Listen to the conversations. Each time you hear the bell, circle the sentence that you think is correct.*

Conversation 1
1. **a)** The man is being pleasant.
   b) The man is being rude.

2. **a)** The man is being pleasant.
   b) The man is being rude.

Conversation 2
1. **a)** The man is ordering a healthy lunch.
   b) The man is ordering an unhealthy lunch.

2. **a)** The man is ordering a healthy lunch.
   b) The man is ordering an unhealthy lunch.

EXERCISE 4

Directions: *You will hear three conversations. At the beginning of each conversation you will hear a question. Listen to the conversation. Then, circle the best answer.*

1. **a)** $50.00
   b) $200.00
   c) $60.00

2. **a)** swimming and dancing
   b) dancing and bike riding
   c) bike riding and basketball

3. **a)** his health and gaining weight
   b) his family and his health
   c) gaining weight and nonsmokers

EXERCISE 5

Directions: Listen to the sentences. Choose the correct vocabulary word.

1. *a)* aerobic
   b) fiber
   c) calorie

2. *a)* stress
   b) poultry
   c) range

3. *a)* shellfish
   b) nutritious
   c) widow

4. *a)* fitness
   b) hole in the wall
   c) genetic

5. *a)* range
   b) lifestyle
   c) genetic

6. *a)* bicycling
   b) stretching
   c) swimming

7. *a)* depressed
   b) vitality
   c) cholesterol

8. *a)* calorie
   b) vitality
   c) kick the habit

9. *a)* serving
   b) poultry
   c) shellfish

10. *a)* reduce
    b) widow
    c) fitness

PART SIX

USING IT: *HOW TO* SPEECHES

Directions: For this assignment, you will demonstrate how to do something for the class. Gather information about your topic (interview experts, go to the library, use the Internet, and so on) and prepare a speech that will help your audience better understand your topic. Be sure to include visual aids in your speech (for example, use charts, diagrams, list of steps, and so on). In your introduction, you might want to include background information about your topic and explain why you chose it. In your conclusion, you might want to point out the best way your audience can use the information you provide.

Possible Topics:

How to perform CPR

How to perform the Heimlich Maneuver

How to administer first aid

How to quit smoking

How to play a sport (basketball, soccer, baseball, tennis, Ping-Pong, and so on)

How to reduce stress

How to prepare a healthy meal

How to meet new friends

How to start a hobby

How to lose weight

CHAPTER THREE

Cruisin' Cross Country

PART ONE

PRE-LISTENING: STATE NAMES

EXERCISE 1A

Using What You Already Know

Directions: *Write the name of the American state or Canadian province next to the abbreviation on Map 1A and Map 1B of the United States and Canada on the next two pages. Refer to the following list of state and province names. The first one, Alabama, has been done for you.*

United States

Alabama	Illinois	Montana	Rhode Island
Alaska	Indiana	Nebraska	South Carolina
Arizona	Iowa	Nevada	South Dakota
Arkansas	Kansas	New Hampshire	Tennessee
California	Kentucky	New Jersey	Texas
Colorado	Louisiana	New Mexico	Utah
Connecticut	Maine	New York	Vermont
Delaware	Maryland	North Carolina	Virginia
District of Columbia (capital)	Massachusetts	North Dakota	Washington
Florida	Michigan	Ohio	West Virginia
Georgia	Minnesota	Oklahoma	Wisconsin
Hawaii	Mississippi	Oregon	Wyoming
Idaho	Missouri	Pennsylvania	

Canada

Alberta	Newfoundland	Prince Edward Island
British Columbia	Nova Scotia	Quebec
Manitoba	Ontario	Saskatchewan
New Brunswick	Ottawa (capital)	

Map 1A This is a map of Canada and the states that border it.

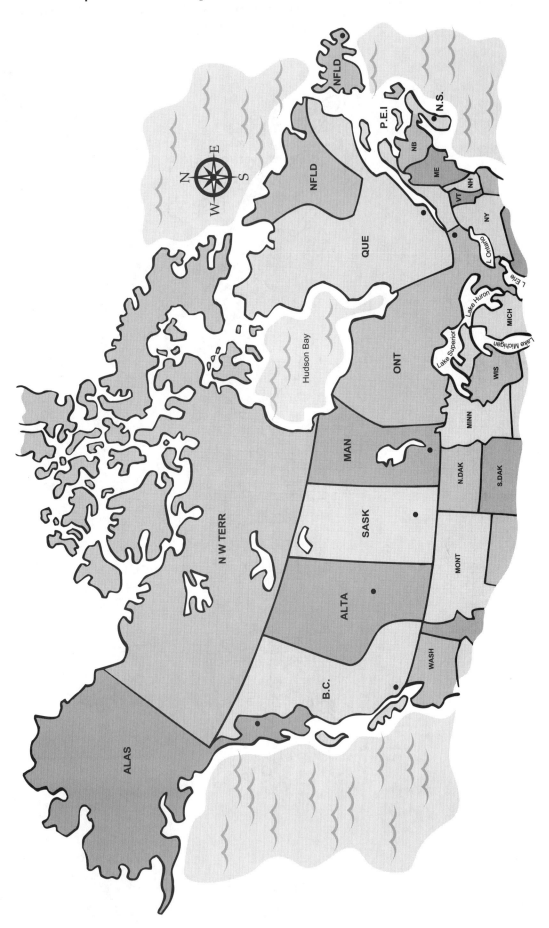

Map 1B This is a map of the *lower 48* states, the Canadian provinces that border them, Hawaii, and part of Mexico. The small map in the right-hand corner gives a complete picture of Alaska, Canada, and the lower 48 states together.

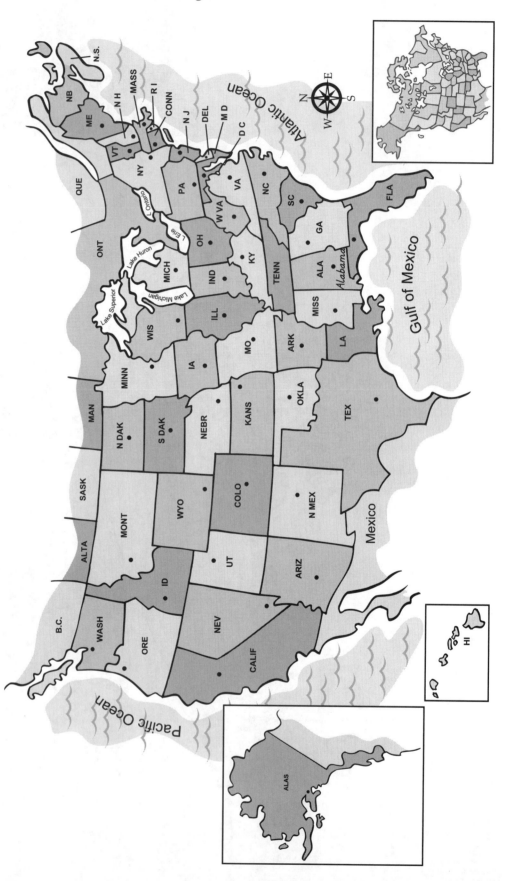

EXERCISE 1B

Directions: Look at Map 1A and Map 1B again to answer the following questions with a partner.

1. Why does West Virginia have the word *west* in its name?

2. What states and provinces are on the Pacific Coast?

3. How many states and provinces have the word *new* in them? Name them.

4. What states and provinces are on the Atlantic Coast?

5. How many states have the word *north* in them? Name them.

6. What is south of the United States?

7. How many states share a border with Canada? Name them.

8. How many states have the word *south* in them? Name them.

9. Which state is separated from the lower 48 states by Canada? Which state isn't located in North America?

10. Find Colorado on your map. If you go from Colorado to Kansas, in which direction are you going? If you go from Colorado to Utah, in which direction are you going? Which state is north of Colorado? Which state is south of Colorado? If you go from Colorado to Nebraska, in which direction are you going? If you go from Colorado to Oklahoma, in which direction are you going?

PART TWO

MAIN DIALOGUE

EXERCISE 1

Scanning for the Main Idea/Background Information

Directions: Listen to the dialogue and try to get a general idea of what is happening. Remember, you don't need to understand everything. Just try to think about the following questions:

1. What is the main idea of this dialogue?
2. Where do you think this dialogue is taking place?
3. How old do you think the speakers are?
4. What do you think their relationship is?
5. Do the speakers sound happy, angry, sad, friendly, unfriendly, sarcastic, annoyed, patient, impatient, or some other way?

EXERCISE 2

Scanning for the Important Points

Directions: Go back to Map 1B. Listen to the dialogue again and draw a line connecting all of the places that Don and Gary plan to visit. Start in L.A. (Note: Don't forget to include the states they pass through but don't visit.)

EXERCISE 3

Vocabulary in Context

Directions: Listen to these sentences from the dialogue and circle the answer that has the same meaning.

1. **a)** It gets too busy.
   b) It gets too hot.

2. **a)** We can make a quick, one-night stop in Salt Lake City.
   b) We should be careful about accidents in Salt Lake City.

3. **a)** Do we have to spend money on a hotel?
   b) Do we have to make a hotel reservation?

4. **a)** They would go many places with us.
   b) They would let us stay with them.

5. **a)** I want to look at the different styles of the buildings.
   b) I want to look at the different kinds of people.

6. **a)** What's the cost of the trip?
   b) What's the schedule of our trip?

7. **a)** I think you drive fast.
   b) I think you drive dangerously.

EXERCISE 4

Scanning for Specific Pieces of Information

Directions: Listen to the dialogue one more time. Then, for each site Don and Gary will visit, fill in the chart on the following page with as much information as you can about the state in which each site is located, including the number of days they plan to stay and the activities they might participate in. (Do not worry about spelling.)

	State	No. of Days	Accommodations	Activities
Grand Canyon				
Salt Lake City			X	X
Yellowstone National Park				
Mt. Rushmore				
Minneapolis				
Chicago				

EXERCISE 5

Directions: In pairs or small groups, look at Map 1A and Map 1B again to discuss these questions:

1. In which states on Gary and Don's trip do they not plan to visit a sight?

2. Fill in your city on the map. How many other cities do you know? Fill them in on the map.

3. How many states do you go through if you take the shortest route from Florida to California? What are they?

4. How many states and provinces do you go through to go from Newfoundland to Illinois by land? What are they? (Be sure to choose the shortest route.)

5. Choose a place you would like to visit. Draw a line from your state to your destination. What states or provinces do you need to go through to get there? (Note: If you are not currently living in the United States, start from Kansas.)

Oral Journal Homework Assignment

Directions: *Prepare a short talk about a place (city, state, country, and so on) you have never visited but would like to see. To help you prepare your outline, use the rough outline that follows.*

I.   Introduction : The place you want to visit
    A. Location
        1. region/geography
        2. climate
    B. How you'll get there
        1. states you'll pass through

II. Accommodations
    A. Where you will stay
        1. hotel/camping/friend's house
        2. length of visit

III. Why you chose this place
    A.
    B.

IV. What you will do there
    A. Famous Sights/Museums
        1.
        2.
        3.
    B. Activities
        1. hiking/biking
        2. tours
    C. Entertainment
        1. nightclubs
        2. performances
        3. sporting events
        4.

V.   Conclusion
    A. How you think the experience will be
    B. Why audience members might consider a similar trip

Don't forget to write a full introduction and conclusion to your speech.

EXERCISE 1A

Section 1 American Regions, Rivers, Mountains, and Lakes

Directions: Listen to the following descriptions of the regions of the United States and fill in the information on Map 2 according to the instructions you hear.

Map 2 The United States

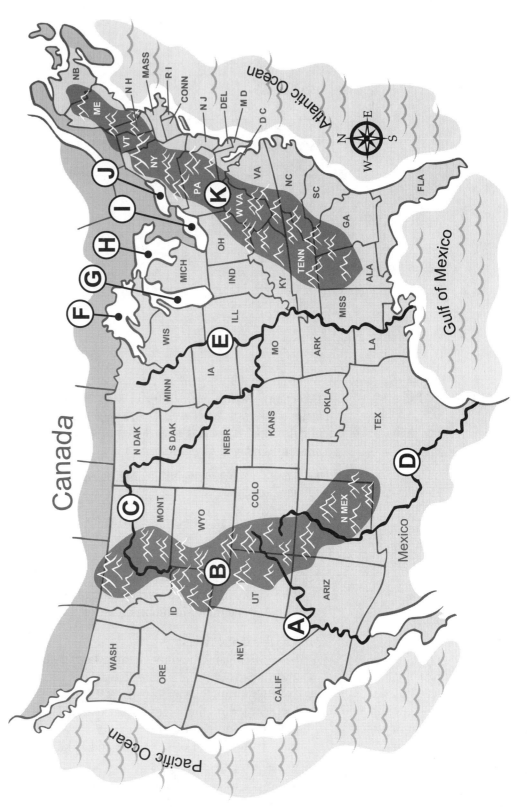

EXERCISE 1B

Directions: Listen to the descriptions of the regions again and fill in the chart with the correct information.

Region	Climate	Major Industries
New England		
Pacific Coast		
Southern		
Middle Atlantic		
Rocky Mountain		
Southwestern		
Midwest		

EXERCISE 1C

Directions: With a partner, fill in Map 2 with the names of the following rivers, mountain ranges, and lakes. Use the clues provided if you need help. Note: Be sure to go in order. The clues in each section depend on the information provided in the previous section.

1. *The four longest rivers* (in order according to length):
    The Missouri
    The Mississippi
    The Rio Grande
    The Colorado

2. *The two biggest mountain ranges:*
    The Rocky Mountains (west of the Mississippi River)
    The Appalachian Mountains (east of the Mississippi River)

3. *The five Great Lakes:*
    Lake Michigan (the only Great Lake not shared by both the United States and Canada)
    Lake Ontario (the smallest Great Lake)
    Lake Superior (the largest Great Lake)
    Lake Erie (north of Ohio)
    Lake Huron (west of Lake Erie and Lake Ontario)

EXERCISE 1D

Directions: Look at Map 2 and listen to the following statements. Decide whether each statement is True or False and circle your answer. (Take notes and refer back to the map if you can't decide right away.)

1. *a)* True
   b) False

2. *a)* True
   b) False

3. *a)* True
   b) False

4. *a)* True
   b) False

5. *a)* True
   b) False

6. *a)* True
   b) False

7. *a)* True
   b) False

8. *a)* True
   b) False

9. *a)* True
   b) False

10. *a)* True
    b) False

Section 2 The Census

Directions: Read and discuss the following information with your instructor.

EXERCISE 2A

population
The number of people living in a particular area

Constitution
The basic law of the United States

House of Representatives
Part of the U.S. government responsible for making laws. Members to the House of Representatives are elected by the people living in each district of the country. States that have a higher population elect more members.

federal
The central government of the U.S.

The census is a complete count of the **population** of the United States. The **Constitution** requires that a census be taken every ten years (always in a year ending in a zero) to decide how many seats each state will have in the United States **House of Representatives**. The information is also used to decide how **federal** money is given to state and local governments, and it helps business and community leaders plan services and improvements for schools, stores, and healthcare services. Areas of the country where the population is higher receive more government money for services, so getting an accurate count of residents is important. Knowing where people live is also necessary for planning emergency services. If, for example, a town is hit by an earthquake, hurricane, flood, or other natural disaster, the area emergency management agencies use census numbers to figure out how many people live in the area and need help. The census is used to provide a picture of each community and its needs.

The census tries to count every person living in the United States, whether or not they are citizens or are here legally. In addition to name, gender, age, race, and marital status, the census form asks questions about housing (whether you own or rent, the size of your home, your rent, the age and condition of the building, how long you've lived there), and other basic personal information (your place of birth, your occupation, your income, and so on). The census form is available in English, Spanish, Chinese, Korean, Tagalog, and Vietnamese, and it is illegal for any information on the form to be given to the police, the FBI, the IRS, the INS, or any other people or agencies.

EXERCISE **2B**

Directions: *With a partner, look at Map 3. This map shows the population of the United States based on census information. Study the map to answer these questions:*

1. Which state has the largest population? Why do you think so many people live there?

2. Which state has the smallest population? Why do you think so few people live there?

3. How many states have a population of 15,000,000 or more?

4. How many states have fewer than 2,000,000 residents?

5. How does the population of California compare with the population of your native state or country?

6. Which state along the Mississippi River has the highest population?

7. Which state along the Missouri River has the smallest population?

8. Four states border Lake Michigan. Which of these states has the smallest population?

9. Which region of the United States has a larger population: the Middle Atlantic states, or the Midwestern states?

10. Which region of the United States has a smaller population: the Southern states, or New England?

Map 3 Population of the United States based on 2000 census data.

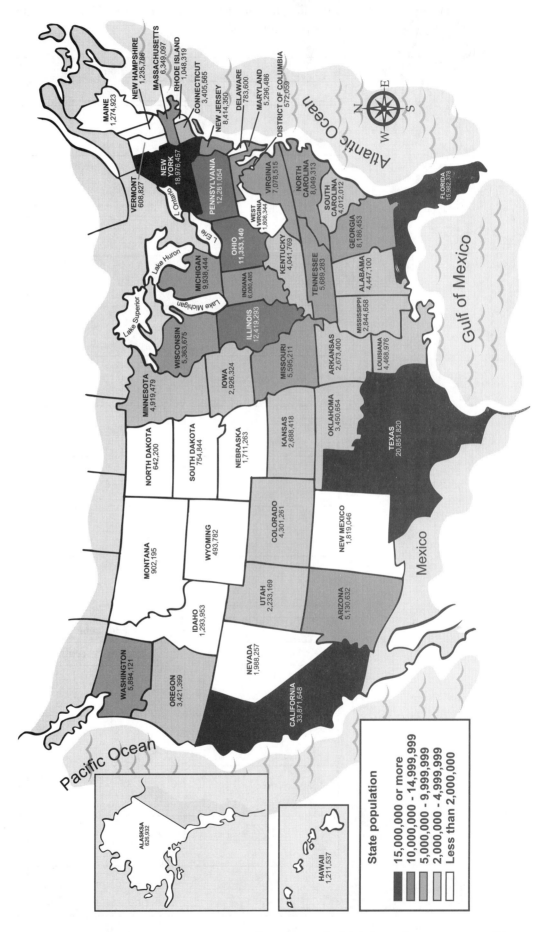

State population

15,000,000 or more
10,000,000 - 14,999,999
5,000,000 - 9,999,999
2,000,000 - 4,999,999
Less than 2,000,000

MAINE 1,274,923
NEW HAMPSHIRE 1,235,786
MASSACHUSETTS 6,349,097
RHODE ISLAND 1,048,319
CONNECTICUT 3,405,565
NEW JERSEY 8,414,350
DELAWARE 783,600
MARYLAND 5,296,486
DISTRICT OF COLUMBIA 572,059
VERMONT 608,827
NEW YORK 18,976,457
PENNSYLVANIA 12,281,054
VIRGINIA 7,078,515
NORTH CAROLINA 8,049,313
SOUTH CAROLINA 4,012,012
FLORIDA 15,982,378
WEST VIRGINIA 1,808,344
OHIO 11,353,140
KENTUCKY 4,041,769
TENNESSEE 5,689,283
GEORGIA 8,186,453
ALABAMA 4,447,100
MICHIGAN 9,938,444
INDIANA 6,080,485
ILLINOIS 12,419,293
MISSISSIPPI 2,844,658
LOUISIANA 4,468,976
WISCONSIN 5,363,675
IOWA 2,926,324
MISSOURI 5,595,211
ARKANSAS 2,673,400
MINNESOTA 4,919,479
NORTH DAKOTA 642,200
SOUTH DAKOTA 754,844
NEBRASKA 1,711,263
KANSAS 2,688,418
OKLAHOMA 3,450,654
TEXAS 20,851,820
MONTANA 902,195
WYOMING 493,782
COLORADO 4,301,261
NEW MEXICO 1,819,046
IDAHO 1,293,953
UTAH 2,233,169
ARIZONA 5,130,632
WASHINGTON 5,894,121
OREGON 3,421,399
NEVADA 1,988,257
CALIFORNIA 33,871,648
ALASKA 626,932
HAWAII 1,211,537

Atlantic Ocean
Gulf of Mexico
Mexico
Pacific Ocean
L. Ontario
L. Erie
Lake Huron
Lake Michigan
Lake Superior

EXERCISE 2C

Directions: Listen to the following student speech about the United States census. As you listen, take notes. Don't forget to use abbreviations and symbols. Use the charts to help organize your notes.

Population		
State	**Year**	**Population**

Education		
Year	**Total or Percent**	**Kind of Degree**

Family		
Year	Total or Percent	Family Information

Directions: With a partner, use your notes from the speech to answer the following questions:

1. What regions of the country had the most residents in 1900?

2. How much did the population of New York State grow between 1900 and 2000? How much did the population of Illinois grow during the same period?

3. How many people do you think were living in California in 1900?

4. What percentage of the population did not have a high school diploma in 1900? In 1940? In 2000?

5. Has the average family size gotten larger or smaller since 1900? Why?

6. What changes occurred in the divorce rate during the 20th century? Why?

7. How do the changes in family size and the divorce rate in the U.S.A. compare with your native country? Explain.

EXERCISE 2E

Directions: *Using your notes and information from Exercise 2C, create an outline for the speech you heard about the census. Make sure you follow proper outline form. Use the guide below to help you.*

I.   Introduction
    A.
    B.
    C.
        1.
        2.
        3.

II. Main Point 1:
    A.
        1.
        2.
        3.
        4.
        5.
    B.
        1.
        2.
        3.
        4.
        5.

III. Main Point 2:
    A.
        1.
        2.
        3.
        4.
        5.

IV. Main Point 3:
    A.
        1.
        2.
        3.
        4.
        5.
        6.
        7.
        8.

V.   Conclusion
    A.
    B.   Predictions
        1.
        2.
        3.

PART FOUR

FOCUS: EXPRESSIONS OF TIME

To show the time that an action occurs, we use time words or phrases such as *last month, the day before yesterday, yesterday, today, now, tomorrow, the day after tomorrow, next year, at six o'clock, in the morning, on Monday, in September, in 1965,* and so on.

In addition, there are other ways of showing when an action happens without naming the specific hour, day, dates, month, or year. With these expressions, we look at the time in relationship to *now*.

Your knowledge of these time words can help you understand when an action takes place even if the speaker doesn't mention the specific hour, day, date, month, or year. As with all other structure clues to meaning, it is important to listen for these time expressions to improve your listening comprehension.

EXERCISE 1

Directions: With your teacher, review the following chart that includes many of these time expressions.

Expression	Time Indicated	Examples
In	(Future tense + *in*) Counting time from now until action starts in the future	Gary and Don will begin their vacation *in* two weeks.
Ago	(Simple past tense + *ago*) Counting time back from now until past action occurred	Gary and Don traveled to Mexico three years *ago*.
For	(Past, Present, or Future + *for*) Counting length of any time	The boys stayed in Vancouver *for* one week. The boys will stay in Chicago *for* three nights.
For Since*	(Present Perfect + *for* or *since*) Counting length of time from beginning of action that began in past and has continued until now	The boys have been planning their trip *for* one month. The boys have been planning their trip *since** April.
Already	(Present Perfect + *already*) Time of action was completed before now	The boys have *already* visited Mexico.
Yet	(Present Perfect Negative + *yet*) Action has not been completed at any time before now	The boys haven't visited Mt. Rushmore *yet*.
Still	(Present tense + *still*) Action happened in past and also happens now	Don and Gary *still* live in Los Angeles.
Anymore	(Negative + *anymore*) Action happened in past, but does not happen now	The boys don't go on vacation with their parents *anymore*.
Within By*	(Future tense + *by* or *within*) Action will be finished before a future time	The boys will return *within* three weeks. The boys will return *by* September 1.*
From X until Y	Total completed duration of time in past or future	The boys will be on vacation *from the beginning of the month until the 30ᵗʰ*.

*Note that with these two expressions a specific hour, day, or date is necessary.

EXERCISE 2

Directions: *Look at the calendar. (Note the word* today *is written on the 14th.) Listen to the following statements to figure out the day or days indicated in each sentence. Write the dates on the blank lines.*

Example   a) *September 13* _____

                  b) *Maybe today. Maybe tomorrow. Maybe Monday.*

1.   *a.* _____

      b. _____

2. _____

3. _____

4.   *a.* _____

      b. _____

5. _____

6. _____

7. _____

8. _____

Sun	Mon	Tues	Wed	Thurs	Fri	Sat
1	2 Labor Day	3	4	5	6	7
8 Grandparents Day	9 Rosh Hashana	10	11	12	13	14 Today
15	16	17 Citizenship Day	18 Yom Kippur	19	20	21
22	23	24	25	26	27	28
29	30					

SEPTEMBER

Flower: Aster / Birthstone: Sapphire

EXERCISE 3

Directions: Listen to the following sentences. Then, circle the sentence that best follows.

1. *a)* The vacation lasted six weeks.
   b) The vacation lasted two months.

2. *a)* It continues to be the largest state.
   b) It was the largest state before, but not now.

3. *a)* They probably want to go there for their vacation.
   b) They probably want to go somewhere else for their vacation.

4. *a)* She can arrive anytime around 9:00 A.M.
   b) She can arrive anytime before 9:00 A.M.

5. *a)* You must wait for that fare.
   b) You can have that fare anytime during the next three weeks.

6. *a)* You must wait for that fare.
   b) You can have that fare anytime during the next three weeks.

7. *a)* I need to make plans.
   b) I don't need to make plans.

8. *a)* We'll get there before the end of five days.
   b) It will take five days to get there.

9. *a)* The population was large before and is now.
   b) The population was large before, but it isn't now.

10. *a)* It was uncommon before, but not now.
    b) It was never uncommon.

PART FIVE

PRACTICE

EXERCISE 1

Directions: You will hear ten questions. Read the three possible responses and circle the correct answer.

1. *a)* Yes, you certainly can.
   b) Call a travel agency.
   c) Go east on Route 40.

2. *a)* No, I'm worried about him.
   b) Yes, he'll come back tomorrow.
   c) Yes, he's still here.

3. *a)* because Hawaiians wanted to be able to vote
   b) That happened in 1960.
   c) Yes, it's the fiftieth state in the United States.

4. *a)* Yes, they do.
   b) Let's look at the map.
   c) all regions except the northeast

5. *a)* about the same as it is today
   b) much lower than it is today
   c) a lot higher before

6. *a)* The most populous state is California.
   b) Family size is much smaller now.
   c) States get important federal money.

7. *a)* only the census bureau
   b) any federal agency
   c) the FBI and INS

8. *a)* They visited Chicago for three days.
   b) They stayed with their aunt and uncle before they went to Chicago.
   c) They decided to head to New York.

9. *a)* My cousin did it in three days.
   b) I have been in Florida for three years.
   c) Florida has one of the longest coasts in the United States.

10. *a)* in the Pacific Coast states
    b) in the New England states
    c) in the Midwestern states

EXERCISE 2

Directions: You will hear ten sentences. Read the three choices and circle the correct answer.

1. *a)* You could do it before, but not now.
   b) You could do it before and now.
   c) You couldn't do it before, but can now.

2. *a)* Iowa is north of Wisconsin.
   b) Iowa is south of Wisconsin.
   c) Iowa is east of Wisconsin.

3. *a)* They made me angry.
   b) They let me stay with them.
   c) They didn't tell me what to do.

4. *a)* You will be able to camp three months from now.
   b) You will not be able to camp three months from now.
   c) You can camp now.

5. *a)* He will cross the Mississippi River.
   b) He will cross the Missouri River.
   c) He will cross the Colorado River.

6. *a)* It is large now.
   b) It was large before.
   c) It was small before.

7. *a)* Illinois still has a large population.
   b) Illinois doesn't have a large population anymore.
   c) Illinois hasn't had a large population since 1900.

8. *a)* They were in Kansas.
   b) They were in Rhode Island.
   c) They were in Colorado.

9. *a)* The Southern states border New England.
   b) New England is south of the Middle Atlantic states.
   c) The Southern States border The Middle Atlantic states.

10. **a)** Fewer people are getting married.
    b) More people are getting high school diplomas.
    c) Fewer people are going to high school.

EXERCISE 3

Directions: Listen to the conversation. Each time you hear the bell, circle the sentence that you think is correct.

1. **a)** The person can speak French.
   b) The person can't speak French.

2. **a)** The person can speak French.
   b) The person can't speak French.

3. **a)** The person likes Montreal.
   b) The person doesn't like Montreal.

4. **a)** The person likes Montreal.
   b) The person doesn't like Montreal.
   c) We don't know.

EXERCISE 4

Directions: You will hear two conversations. At the beginning of each conversation, you will hear a question. Listen to the conversation. Then, circle the best answer.

1. **a)** the Pacific Coast states
   b) the Southern states
   c) the Northeastern states

2. **a)** the Midwest
   b) New England
   c) the Southwest

EXERCISE 5

Directions: Listen to the sentences. Choose the correct vocabulary word.

1. **a)** Boil
   b) Population
   c) Federal

2. **a)** Constitution
   b) Architecture
   c) Itinerary

3. **a)** House of Representatives
   b) Census
   c) Accommodations

4. **a)** Climate
   b) Customs
   c) Economy

5. **a)** Crash for a night
   b) Province
   c) Region

6. **a)** Region
   b) Symphony
   c) Architecture

7. **a)** Border
   b) Spring for
   c) Census

8. **a)** State
   b) Province
   c) Customs

9. **a)** Crash for a night
   b) Put me up
   c) Burn rubber

10. **a)** Federal
    b) Geography
    c) Census

PART SIX

USING IT: PLANNING A VACATION

Directions: For this assignment, you and a partner are going to plan a trip to a location at least three days away from where you live. You will show the class your itinerary for a road trip (driving to the destination). You need to plan a trip that will last at least three nights. You should plan for your speech to be about five minutes long, so don't make your itinerary too long or too short. You and your partner will need to do some research to answer these questions:

- Why did you choose this destination?
- How long will your trip take?
- What will your itinerary be?
- Which sights will you visit along the way?
- Where will you sleep in each city or town that you visit?
- How much money do you think you'll need for the trip?

To get information for your presentation, you can visit a travel agency, look at travel books in the bookstore, get information in the library, use the Internet, and/or interview people who are familiar with the cities/states you plan to visit. If you or someone you know is a member of an automobile association (for example, AAA), you can get free maps and books with important information about your destination. This is what you need to find out:

Travel Time:

How long will it take you to drive to your destination? How far will you go each day?

Itinerary:

Where will you stop the first day/night? Why did you choose this place? Where will you stop the second day/night? Why did you choose this place?

Accommodations:

Where will you stay? Find the names of hotels in the cities you will be traveling to/through. There are many national hotel chains (Days Inn, Hyatt, and so on) that have toll-free phone numbers. You can also visit their websites to find out how much a room costs, whether the hotel has a restaurant, if there is parking available, and so on.

Sights of Interest:

What will you see in the places you choose to visit? Describe what is interesting about each place, what people can do there, what hours it is open, and how much it costs.

The goal of your speech is to convince your classmates to take the trip that you describe. You should bring in maps, pictures, and other things that will help get your audience interested in your itinerary. You can also create charts with important information such as the prices of things, schedules, and so on. Remember, your speech should not be more than five minutes long, so don't try to do too much. Also, you and your partner need to share the responsibility for all aspects of this project. You should both do the research, prepare the outline, and practice together.

Look at the sample outline to give you an idea of how to organize your speech information. Discuss the outline with your instructor.

Our Road Trip

I. Introduction
   A. A brief overview of trip
   B. Why you chose your route/destination

II. Itinerary
   A. First stop
      1. Description of place
         a. Size/population
         b. Weather
      2. Accommodations
         a. Where you will stay
         b. How much it will cost
      3. Places of interest
         a. What to see/do
         b. Transportation to places of interest
         c. Cost
   B. Second stop
      1. Description of place
         a. Size/population
         b. Weather
      2. Accommodations
         a. Where you will stay
         b. How much it will cost
      3. Places of interest
         a. What to see/do
         b. Transportation to places of interest
         c. Cost
   C. Third stop
      1. Description of place
         a. Size/population
         b. Weather
      2. Accommodations
         a. Where you will stay
         b. How much it will cost
      3. Places of interest
         a. What to see/do
         b. Transportation to places of interest
         c. Cost

III. Conclusion
   A. Summary of itinerary
   B. Reasons you recommend this trip

4

What's My Line?

PART ONE

PRE-LISTENING: WHAT'S IN AN INTERVIEW?

Using What You Already Know

EXERCISE 1

Directions: Pretend that you are going to conduct an interview in English about someone's college major or job. In pairs or small groups, discuss how you would do it. Answer these questions.

1. What would you do beforehand to prepare for the interview?

2. What is a good way to begin the interview?

3. What are some ways for you to remember the information you get during the interview?

4. What should you do if you don't understand something the **informant** says?

5. How can you show the informant that you understand what s/he is saying?

6. What is a good way to end an interview?

informant
The person you are interviewing

EXERCISE 2

Directions: Now, write a list of questions that you might use to interview someone about her/his college major or occupation. After completing your list, each group should write its list on the chalkboard. As a class, decide which list of questions would work the best.

1. _____

2. _____

3. _____

4. _____

5. _____

6. _____

7. _____

8. _____

9. _____

10. _____

PART TWO

MAIN DIALOGUE

Scanning for the Main Idea/Background Information

Directions: Listen to the dialogue and try to get a general idea of what is happening. Remember, you don't need to understand everything. Just try to answer the following questions:

1. What is the main idea of this dialogue?
2. Where do you think this dialogue is taking place?
3. What is the relationship between the two speakers?
4. How old do you think the speakers are?
5. How would you describe the two speakers?

Scanning for the Important Points

Directions: Now, listen to the dialogue again to answer these questions:

1. At what time of the year does this interview take place?

2. How long does it usually take a student to finish the retail floristry certificate program?

3. Why is the informant interested in the program?

4. What kind of jobs can you get with a certificate in retail floristry?

5. Does the informant think her classes are difficult? Explain.

6. What are some of the important classes you need to take if you study retail floristry?

7. What are some other classes a retail floristry student might want to take?

8. Why does the informant think that the UFS program is good?

9. What does she think is bad about the program?

10. What suggestions does the informant have for foreign students who take classes in retail floristry?

Scanning for Specific Pieces of Information

Directions: *Listen to the dialogue one more time. This time, listen for the questions the interviewer asks and write down as many questions as you can. Do not try to copy each question word-for-word. Just take notes to help you remember the main idea of each question.*

_____

_____

_____

_____

_____

_____

_____

_____

_____

_____

_____

_____

_____

_____

EXERCISE 4

Now, in pairs or small groups, compare your questions. Decide as a group which questions were the most important in the interview. How many were the same as the ones you wrote for Exercise 2 in Part One?

Vocabulary in Context

Directions: *Listen to these sentences from the dialogue and circle the answers that have the same meaning.*

1. *a)* the cost it takes to do something
    b) the time it takes to do something

2. *a)* Why was it interesting?
    b) Why was it beautiful?

3. *a)* I'm successful with plants and flowers.
    b) I'm allergic to plants and flowers.

4. **a)** I'm having a hard time.
   b) I'm doing well.

5. **a)** classes that teach you how to grow plants
   b) classes that teach you how to label plants

6. **a)** helpful
   b) unnecessary

7. **a)** things you learn from a book
   b) things you learn from doing

8. **a)** looking at only good points
   b) looking at good and bad points

9. **a)** to do something with your hands
   b) to do something successfully

10. **a)** have an easy time
    b) have a difficult time

EXERCISE 5

Directions: In pairs or small groups, discuss the following questions.

1. Do you think the interview was a success? Explain.

2. What small problem did the informant have during the interview? How did she handle it? What would you do in this situation? Explain.

3. Where do you think the interviewer is from? Why?

4. Is there anything that you would have changed about this interview?

5. Are there any ideas that you got from this interview that will help you when you conduct an interview? Explain.

Oral Journal Homework Assignment

Directions: Pretend that you could conduct an interview with any famous person, living or dead. Describe your choice, why you chose her/him, and what you'd like to find out in the interview. Use the following outline to help you prepare your talk.

I. Introduction: The person you've chosen
   A. Person's identity
      1. what s/he is famous for
      2. how you know about him/her
   B. What you would talk about: the interview you would like to have

II. *Brief* Background Info about Famous Person
   A. Birth date, birth place, nationality
   B. Greatest achievements
      1.
      2.
      3.

III. Why You Chose the Person
    A. Influence s/he has had on you
        1.
        2.
    B. Importance of person
        1.
        2.

IV. What You Would Ask this Person
    A. Topic 1
        1. question
        2. reason for question
    B. Topic 2
        1. question
        2. reason for question
    C. Topic 3
        1. question
        2. reason for question

V. Conclusion
    A. Summary of what this experience would be like
    B. How conducting this interview would change your life

Be careful! The topic for this speech is an *interview* with a famous person. Your focus must be on the interview: why you chose this person, what you would learn from this person, and how the interview would change your life. Do *not* simply prepare a speech about the life of a famous person. While some biographical information is appropriate, the speech should focus on the interview, so try not to include more than 20 percent biographical facts.

Remember that the topic is just about an interview that you would like to have. You do not know what your informant would say, so do not make up answers for your informant. Simply explain what you would like to learn from this person, why you would like to know it, and how it would affect you.

PART THREE

EXPANSION: RULES FOR GOOD INTERVIEWS

EXERCISE 1

conduct
To hold, direct, or lead
approach
To speak to someone for the
first time
assure
To promise

cue
A signal

Directions: In pairs or small groups, study the list of Rules for Good Interviews. Discuss what each rule means and why it is important for good interviews.

Rule 1: Pick a safe place to **conduct** your interview.

Rule 2: Be sure the place you choose has informants who can answer your interview topic questions.

Rule 3: When you **approach** people, make sure that you are friendly and respectful. **Assure** them that you won't take up too much of their time.

Rule 4: Always prepare your questions in advance and make sure to practice asking them before your interview. Organize your questions from general to specific.

Rule 5: Begin your interview by asking warm-up questions to help the informant feel comfortable.

Rule 6: Maintain good eye contact during the interview, and show your informant that you are interested by using appropriate verbal and nonverbal **cues.**

Rule 7: Take good notes during the interview. Try to use abbreviations and symbols to help you.

Rule 8: Be sure to ask for clarification if you don't understand something the informant says.

Rule 9: Use good follow-up questions to get more information during your interview.

Rule 10: Remember to thank your informant.

EXERCISE 2

Directions: Pretend you are going to conduct an interview. In pairs or small groups, answer these questions:

1. If the interview topic were about childcare problems, where would a good place be to find informants? Which places would not be helpful?

2. What are some things you could say to introduce yourself and ask permission for an interview?

3. Write down a couple of warm-up questions. Try to think of one or two questions that would be especially good today (for example, ask about today's weather, or a current event topic).

4. Choose a topic of interest to all group members, such as: eating habits, hobbies, entertainment. Then, as a group, write seven interview questions for that topic. Be sure to start with general questions and move to more specific ones.

5. Now, find a partner who was not in your group. Take turns interviewing each other using your topic and questions. Remember:
- Begin the interview with a good introduction and warm-up question.
- Maintain eye contact with your informant.
- Use good verbal and nonverbal cues.
- Take good notes using symbols and abbreviations.
- Ask for clarification when you don't understand something.
- Make sure you ask at least one follow-up question during your interview.

EXERCISE 3

Directions: *Listen to the following portions of interviews. In each interview, one of the Rules for Good Interviewing is being broken. Take notes as you listen and write down what you think each interviewer is doing wrong. Then, in small groups, discuss ways the interviewers could do a better job. (Note that some of these portions are in the middle of the interview.)*

1. Problem:

Solution:

2. Problem:

Solution:

3. Problem:

Solution:

4. Problem:

Solution:

5. Problem:

Solution:

PART FOUR

FOCUS: USING STRESS FOR CLARIFICATION

All languages use stress and intonation to add meaning to sentences. Stress usually means that a word has a rising change in pitch and an increase in loudness and length.

Stress is used in all sentences to indicate the most important words. However, when the stress of a sentence is particularly strong or when the primary (the most important) stress is moved to a different word, the speaker is indicating special meaning.

One of the meanings that strong stress indicates is a need for clarification. When a speaker is not sure that he or she has correctly understood something, the speaker will repeat what he or she has just heard and stress the word or words that are confusing. She or he will use a rising intonation as a way of asking for clarification.

Listen to the dialogue.

As you heard, the interviewer stressed the words *ten hours* to indicate that he wasn't sure he understood that information and needed clarification. The informant, therefore, supplied confirmation that the interviewer, indeed, correctly understood *ten hours*.

EXERCISE 1

Directions: *Listen to the following sentences, and underline the word or phrase with the greatest stress in each sentence.*

1. Lawyers commonly work for no money?

2. A pre-med student can major in any field?

3. Full-time students take fifteen units?

4. Students are required to pay a fee for activities?

5. A travel agent gets free airfare?

6. To get into the State University, you need 1200?

7. You apprentice for two years?

8. A history or psychology class?

9. No reimbursement for supplies?

10. Always use drama?

EXERCISE 2

Directions: Listen to the following short dialogues, and choose the sentence that would best follow each one in a normal dialogue. Circle the correct answer.

Example: 1. *ⓐ)* Yes, they write their lesson plans.
      b) Yes, most teachers do.

The correct answer is *a* because the speaker stressed the word *busy.*

Example: 2. *a)* Yes, they write their lessons plans.
      ⓑ) Yes, most teachers do.

The correct answer is *b* because the speaker stressed the word *teachers.*

1. *a)* Yeah. It's really a common practice.
  b) Yeah. They do it for free.

2. *a)* Yes. Pre-med.
  b) Yes. Any field.

3. *a)* Right. That's for full-time students.
  b) Right. Fifteen units.

4. *a)* Yup. They have no choice.
  b) Yup. All students.

5. *a)* Yes, and so do airline workers.
  b) Yes, he goes for free.

6. *a)* Yeah, State U.
  b) Yeah, 1200.

7. *a)* That's right. You work for no pay.
  b) That's right. You do it for two years.

8. *a)* Yeah. Only one is necessary.
  b) Yeah. Psychology can be very helpful.

9. *a)* Uh-huh. You know, for things like paints, canvasses, and brushes.
  b) Uh-huh. No money at all.

10. *a)* Every minute he is on the job.
   b) Drama is an important sales tool.

PART FIVE

PRACTICE

Directions: *You will hear ten questions. Read the three possible responses and circle the correct answer.*

1. **a)** I want to get a job there.
   b) It's beneficial to my career.
   c) I started working there last year.

2. **a)** with a follow-up question
   b) with an information question
   c) with a warm-up question

3. **a)** Begin the interview with a good introduction.
   b) Use good verbal and nonverbal cues.
   c) Be sure to thank her/him at the end of the interview.

4. **a)** an international school
   b) a senior citizen center
   c) a fast-food restaurant

5. **a)** before the interview
   b) during the interview
   c) after the interview

6. **a)** in a local cafe
   b) in your kitchen
   c) in a lecture class

7. **a)** Be friendly and respectful.
   b) Take notes.
   c) Practice your questions in advance.

8. **a)** Yes, she only works mornings.
   b) Yes, I work more hours than she does.
   c) Yes, she makes more money than I do.

9. **a)** ten miles from my house
   b) about 15 minutes by bus
   c) since 1997

10. **a)** A Spanish or Italian class might help.
    b) You need at least thirty units of French.
    c) I'd like to live and work in Paris some day.

Directions: *You will hear ten sentences. Read the three choices and choose the correct answer.*

1. **a)** She was absent the day of the test.
   b) She should have studied harder.
   c) She feels satisfied with her results.

2. **a)** He has many different job offers.
   b) He is probably looking for work every day.
   c) He is having trouble finding a job.

3. *a)* He should have prepared his questions in advance.
   b) He should have asked for clarification.
   c) He should have maintained eye contact.

4. *a)* His rose garden is beautiful.
   b) He should probably grow something else.
   c) He likes to grow green roses.

5. *a)* Was it a certificate program?
   b) Was it in 1999?
   c) Is that when you finished?

6. *a)* He asked the informant to explain the word.
   b) He asked the informant to spell the word.
   c) He asked the informant to pronounce the word.

7. *a)* Is it normal?
   b) Is it software developers?
   c) Is it a 60-hour week?

8. *a)* She became vice president first.
   b) She became vice president in May, 1998.
   c) She got her degree first.

9. *a)* Dental hygienists need a certificate.
   b) Dental hygienists need an associate's degree.
   c) Both jobs require an associate's degree.

10. *a)* Was it the chairperson?
    b) Was it the anthropology department?
    c) Was it anatomy?

EXERCISE 3

Directions: Listen to the conversation. Each time you hear the bell, circle the sentence that you think is correct.

1. *a)* She has a college degree.
   b) She doesn't have a college degree.

2. *a)* She has a college degree.
   b) She doesn't have a college degree.

3. *a)* She is applying for a job as a legal assistant.
   b) She is applying for a job as a secretary.

4. *a)* She is applying for a job as a legal assistant.
   b) She is applying for a job as a secretary.

5. *a)* She has a college degree.
   b) She doesn't have a college degree.

6. *a)* She should be hired.
   b) She shouldn't be hired.

EXERCISE 4

Directions: You will hear two conversations. At the beginning of each conversation, you will hear a question. Listen to the conversation. Then, circle the best answer.

1. *a)* proud
    b) angry
    c) disappointed

2. *a)* being friendly
    b) asking for clarification
    c) asking follow-up questions

EXERCISE 5

Directions: Listen to the sentences. Choose the correct vocabulary word.

1. *a)* follow-up question
    b) information question
    c) warm-up question

2. *a)* green thumb
    b) attracted to
    c) beneficial

3. *a)* at the rate I'm going
    b) can't handle
    c) practical experience

4. *a)* practical experience
    b) evaluates
    c) aces

5. *a)* It wasn't difficult.
    b) It was a little difficult.
    c) It was very difficult.

6. *a)* information question
    b) clarification question
    c) follow-up question

7. *a)* beneficial
    b) friendly
    c) assured

8. *a)* conducted
    b) promised
    c) breezed through

9. *a)* warm-up
    b) approach
    c) eye contact

10. *a)* assure
    b) occupation
    c) informant

PART SIX

USING IT: INTERVIEW PROJECT

Section 1 Interview Preparation

Directions: For this assignment, you will interview a native English speaker. Choose one of these topics:

• College major
• Occupation

Follow these steps:

Step 1: With your instructor, decide on a due date for this assignment.

Step 2: Write the questionnaire. Be sure to include a good warm-up question along with your content questions about the topic. Either type or carefully hand print your questionnaire. Leave several lines of space after each question for your informant's answers. Have your teacher approve your questions before going to Step 3.

Step 3: Conduct the interview. Be sure to follow the Rules for Good Interviews discussed in this chapter. During the interview, take notes on a separate piece of paper (do not write your answers on the questionnaire yet).

Step 4: After the interview is completed, use your notes to fill in your questionnaire with the answers from the interview. Be sure to include any follow-up questions. Make sure that it's easy to see the difference between your questions and the informant's answers by using tags such as:

Interviewer:

Informant:

Section 2 Interview Feedback

EXERCISE 1

Directions: In small groups, compare your interview results and answer the following questions:

1. Where did you find your informant? Would you choose this place again? Why/why not?

2. What was your warm-up question? Did it help to make your informant more comfortable?

3. Which question that you asked was the best? Why? Which question was not very good? Why not?

4. Talk a little bit about your informant. What is her/his major or occupation? Why did s/he choose it, and so on.

5. What was the most interesting thing you learned from your informant?

6. What will you do differently the next time you interview someone?

EXERCISE 2

Directions: In your group, discuss the questions in the chart. For each question, you will tally (count) the number of yes *and* no *answers that group members give. Mark your tallies in the* yes *and* no *columns in the chart.*

Questions	Yes	No
1. Were you scared before the interview?		
2. Did you need to ask more than one person before someone agreed to be your informant?		
3. Would you like to be friends with your informant?		
4. Did you enjoy your interview?		
5. Does your informant's major/occupation interest you?		
6. Will you feel less scared the next time you do an interview?		

EXERCISE 3

Directions: *Using your tallies from Exercise 2, prepare a graph to show your group's results. A graph is a special kind of drawing that presents data (information) in an easy-to-read way. There are many different kinds of graphs, and for this assignment, you will make a bar graph, which uses bars to represent data. To make a bar graph, draw bars for the total number of yes and no answers for each question. Here is an example of a bar graph:*

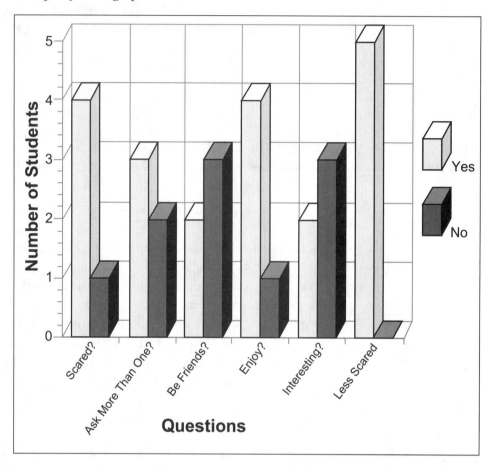

EXERCISE 4

Directions: *As a class, combine all group statistics and make a final bar graph that includes everyone's data. Then, analyze the results using the following questions:*

1. Looking at the graph (the statistical information), which questions provide the most helpful information about the experience? How can you tell?

2. Looking at the graph (the statistical information), which questions provide the least helpful information about the experience? How can you tell?

3. Do any of the results shock you? Why?

4. Are any of the results what you would have expected? Why?

5. What conclusions can you draw from the information in the graph? For example, is it true that most ESL/EFL students are scared when they have to conduct an intereview? If the answer is yes, what are the reasons? What other conclusions can you draw from your graph?

CHAPTER   FIVE

Face the Issues

77

PART ONE

PRE-LISTENING: WHAT WORRIES YOU THE MOST?

Using What You Already Know

Modern life is not always easy. Many people are concerned or worried about the issues that face our society today. We depend upon our leaders (mayors, governors, the president, and so on) to help us solve these social problems.

EXERCISE 1

Directions: *Look at the following list of issues and decide which one concerns you the most at this point in your life. Also, try to think of things that could or should be done that would make you feel less concerned or worried about the issue you have chosen.*

Drugs	Gang Violence	Hunger	AIDS
Unemployment	Taxes	Racism	Pollution
Homelessness	Education	Illegal Immigrants	Campaign Reform
Political Corruption	Energy Crisis	Water Issues	Welfare System
Health Care	Housing	Other: _____	

EXERCISE 2

Directions: *In small groups, share the issue you chose and explain why you have chosen this particular problem. Discuss possible solutions.*

PART TWO

MAIN DIALOGUE

EXERCISE 1

Scanning for the Main Idea/Background Information

Directions: *Listen to the selection and try to get a general idea of what is happening. Remember, you don't need to understand everything. Just try to think about the following questions:*

1. What is the main idea of this selection?

2. Where do you think the speakers are?

3. What is the relationship between the speakers?

4. How old do you think the speakers are?

5. How do you think each speaker's voice sounds (professional, reasonable, rude, harsh, and so on)?

liberal
Supporting political ideas that include more involvement by the government in people's lives

conservative
Supporting political ideas that include less involvement by the government in people's lives

Scanning for the Important Points

Directions: Now, listen to the dialogue again to answer these questions:

1. What office are the two candidates running for?

2. What jobs do the two candidates have?

3. What is the first issue the candidates discussed?

4. What is the second issue the candidates discussed?

5. What is the third issue the candidates discussed?

6. How would you describe the two candidates: Politically **liberal**, **conservative**, and so on?

EXERCISE 3

Scanning for Specific Pieces of Information

Directions: Look at the issues in the following chart. Then, listen to the dialogue one more time. As you listen, put a check (✔) next to the candidate who would agree with each issue.

	Issue	Bella Porter	Dan Shmankie
1.	Candidate believes that job training and affordable housing will help the homeless.		
2.	Candidate believes that many homeless people belong in jail.		
3.	Candidate believes that homeless people hurt tourist business.		
4.	Candidate believes that government money does not solve society problems.		
5.	Candidate believes that low test scores are the result of bad teachers.		
6.	Candidate believes that teachers should work harder to get raises.		
7.	Candidate believes that schools should be run like a successful business.		
8.	Candidate believes that, in order to get the best teachers, salaries should be raised.		
9.	Candidate believes that government has no business telling landlords how much rent to charge.		
10.	Candidate says that 56% of the poor and elderly cannot afford to live in the city.		

Vocabulary in Context

Directions: Listen to these sentences from the selection and circle the answer that has the same meaning.

1. *a)* led to agreement
   b) led to argument

2. *a)* to hide a problem
   b) to fix a problem

3. *a)* asked in a polite way
   b) asked in a frightening way

4. *a)* go up
   b) go down

5. *a)* making many of the same things
   b) making many things poorly

6. *a)* not enough supplies
   b) not enough time

7. *a)* in favor of
   b) against

8. *a)* growing slowly
   b) growing quickly

Directions: In pairs or small groups, discuss the following questions. Then, as a class, compare your answers.

1. For each of the issues discussed in the selection, decide which candidate you agree with. Explain your reasons.

2. How do you think the two candidates would feel about other issues you have discussed in this chapter?

3. Dan Shmankie said, "Some of my best friends are teachers." Does this mean he really wants to help teachers? Explain your answer.

4. Which of the two candidates would you vote for? Why?

Oral Journal Homework Assignment

Directions: Prepare a short talk about your greatest concern. You may choose one of the issues from the first exercise in this chapter, or choose any other issue that worries you the most. To help you prepare your speech, use the rough outline below.

I. Introduction: Your Greatest Concern
   A. How long you have had the concern
   B. How your concern began

II. Reasons this Issue Is Important
   A.
      1.
      2.
   B.
      1.
      2.
   C.
      1.
      2.

III. Possible Solutions to This Problem
   A.
      1.
   B.
      1.

IV. Conclusion
   A. Warning—if problem is not solved
   B. How audience can become involved

PART THREE

EXPANSION

Section 1 The United States Government

EXERCISE 1

Directions: With a partner, read the following to answer the questions.

The government of the United States of America is a unique system made up of several layers including local, state, and federal. As you learned in Chapter Three, the United States is made up of fifty separate states. Each state in turn is made up of many counties, cities, towns, and villages. What makes the U.S. different from many other democratic countries in the world is the amount of power that state governments have within their borders. Each of the fifty states is allowed to decide for itself many issues, such as education, state taxes, business laws, and public services. Both **federal** and state governments in the United States are made up of three branches (major parts): **executive**, **legislative**, and **judicial**.

federal
The government in Washington, D.C.

executive
The presidential branch of government

legislative
The law making branch of government

judicial
The law judging branch of government

settlers
The first Europeans to form their own communities in North America

colonies
New communities started by the settlers in North America

Constitution
The highest laws and rules of the United States

The power that the states have is the result of the early history of the United States. When the first **settlers** arrived in North America in the 1600s, the **colonies** they established had their own governments and sets of laws. This is because the colonies were very different from each other. Some colonies had strong religious beliefs and systems, and other colonies were based on business and industry. Each colony created its own government to take care of its unique needs. Later, when the United States was formed, the writers of the U.S. **Constitution** created a federal government to oversee national issues, such as defense, money regulation, and foreign relations. The federal government has the most power in the U.S. but still allows each of the fifty states to make many of its own decisions.

1. How is the United States government different from many other governments?

2. What is the difference between the state and federal governments in the U.S.?

3. What is similar between the state and federal governments in the U.S.?

4. Why do state governments have so much power?

5. Do you think it's a good idea for state governments to have so much power? Why/why not?

EXERCISE 2

Directions: *Listen to the following lecture about the three branches of the U.S. government to answer the following True/False questions.*

1.	All branches of the federal government have the same powers.	**True**	**False**
2.	*Checks and balances* is the banking system of the U.S.	**True**	**False**
3.	The president is in charge of the executive branch.	**True**	**False**
4.	The president makes the laws of the country.	**True**	**False**
5.	A president can serve for eight years.	**True**	**False**
6.	The president can veto a law that Congress passes.	**True**	**False**
7.	The House of Representatives has two representatives from each state.	**True**	**False**
8.	Senators are elected for six-year terms.	**True**	**False**
9.	There are two senators from Iowa.	**True**	**False**
10.	When the president vetoes a bill, it cannot become law.	**True**	**False**
11.	Congress collects the sales tax for each state.	**True**	**False**
12.	The Supreme Court justices are elected by the people.	**True**	**False**
13.	The Supreme Court makes sure that legal decisions are correct according to the United States Constitution.	**True**	**False**
14.	The U.S. is the only country in the world with three branches of government.	**True**	**False**

Directions: Listen to the lecture one more time. While you are listening, take notes. Then, fill in the following outline. (Note: You may want to add or delete numbers or letters.) When you are finished, compare your outlines and discuss them as a class.

I.   Introduction

    A.   _____

        1.

        2.

        3.

    B.   _____

II. The Executive Branch

    A.   The president's power

        1.

        2.

        3.

        4.

        5.

    B.   Who can become president

        1.

        2.

        3.

    C.   Terms of office

        1.

III. The Legislative Branch: _____

    A.   The Senate

        1.

        2.

        3.

B. The House of Representatives

    1.

    2.

    3. Number based on population

       a.

C. The responsibilities of Congress

    1. Making laws

       a.

       b.

    2.

    3.

    4.

IV. The Judicial Branch

A. The federal courts

    1.

    2.

B. The Supreme Court

    1.

    2.

    3.

V. Conclusion

EXERCISE 4

Directions: In pairs or small groups, discuss these questions.

1. Do you think the idea of three branches of government is a good one? Why/why not?

2. How is the government of your country similar to the US government? Describe and explain.

3. What do you like about the U.S. system of government? Explain.

4. What do you not like about the U.S. system of government? Explain.

Section 2 The State of the Union Address

EXERCISE 1

Directions: With a partner, read the following to answer the questions.

The United States Constitution says that the president must give a report to Congress every year in which he or she talks about how the country is doing. This speech is called the *State of the Union Address* and is given to Congress at the beginning of the year. In the State of the Union Address, the president talks about which programs are working well, and which ones need to be improved. The president may also use the State of the Union Address to talk about which national problems he or she feels are important to take care of in the coming year. The president also suggests to Congress which laws should be made to take care of these problems. Of course, the senators and representatives who listen to the president's address may or may not do what the president suggests. Because it is independent, Congress can either listen to or ignore what the president says during the State of the Union address. But, many Americans watch the State of the Union Address very carefully to find out what the president thinks is important for the United States. If the president talks about an idea that has become very popular in the country, the members of Congress may feel that they have to also talk about it in the Senate and House of Representatives. So, the State of the Union Address is a very important yearly speech.

1. Who gives the State of the Union Address? Why?

2. When is the State of the Union Address given?

3. Who is the audience for the State of the Union Address?

4. What is the topic of the State of the Union Address?

5. Why is the State of the Union Address an important speech?

Directions: *Listen to part of President Eleanor Sullivan-Carver's State of the Union Address. Each time you hear the bell, write down the issue that the president is discussing.*

1. _____

2. _____

3. _____

4. _____

5. _____

EXERCISE 3

Directions: *Read the list of proposals. Some of the proposals were mentioned in President Sullivan-Carver's speech, and some were not. Listen to the speech again. Each time you hear the bell, decide which proposals were suggested for each issue. Write the letters in the chart.*

A. Reduce the number of students in grade school classrooms.
B. Help families build houses.
C. Provide more childcare.
D. Lower the unemployment rate.
E. Reduce taxes to help families pay for childcare.
F. Provide healthcare coverage for more children.
G. Hire more police officers.
H. Make all teachers take tests every year to show they can teach.
I. Pass a law that checks all new handgun owners.
J. Give senior citizens a tax refund.
K. Increase taxes for large families.
L. Give women more training for computer-related jobs.
M. Make sure people are paid the same salary for the same work.
N. Pay teachers more money.
O. Make automobile license laws stronger.

Issue	Proposal
Issue 1	
Issue 2	
Issue 3	
Issue 4	
Issue 5	

PART FOUR

FOCUS: CHANGES IN MEANING THROUGH STRESS AND PITCH

As we learned in Chapter Four, stress usually means that a word has a rising change in pitch and an increase in loudness and length. In that lesson we learned that strong stress sometimes indicates a need for clarification. When speakers are not sure that they have correctly understood something, they will repeat what they have just heard, stress the word or words that they are confused about, and use a rising intonation as a way of asking for clarification.

Strong stress on a specific word or phrase can also indicate that a sentence has a different meaning from the exact same sentence which has strong stress on another word or phrase. In this case, speakers use stress to correct something that was just said.

Listen to the following three sentences that have the exact same words. Notice that in each sentence the stress is on a different word or phrase. Pay close attention to how the meaning of each sentence changes because of the difference in stress, even though all three sentences have the same words.

1. **Speaker 1:** Bella Porter gave a powerful speech at the debate without any preparation.

   Speaker 2: Bella Porter **PLANNED** her speech for the debate.

   The stress on *planned* indicates that she didn't just speak off the top of her head.

2. **Speaker 1:** Dan Shmankie planned a powerful speech for the debate.

   Speaker 2: **BELLA PORTER** planned her speech for the debate.

   The stress on *Bella Porter* indicates that it was not another person, such as Dan Shmankie.

3. **Speaker 1:** Bella Porter planned her speech for a TV commercial.

   Speaker 2: Bella Porter planned her speech for the **DEBATE**.

   The stress on *debate* indicates that the speech was not planned for a TV commercial.

In addition to stress, the pitch, (the rising and falling of the stressed word) also helps to clearly indicate differences in meaning when words or sentences are the same. In these situations, however, the different pitches reflect different feelings or emotions. Here is an example of how differences in pitch can indicate different emotions. In all three cases, the answer to the question, *How did you like the movie?* is the same: *Great.* The different pitch in each answer, however, greatly changes the meaning of each answer.

1. **Speaker 1:** How did you like the movie?

   Speaker 2: Great.

   The pitch goes down in a normal rising-falling pattern showing a rather neutral opinion or neutral feelings about the movie.

2. **Speaker 1:** How did you like the movie?

   Speaker 2: Great!

   The pitch starts at the highest level and falls sharply showing a very enthusiastic opinion or excited feelings about the movie.

3. **Speaker 1:** How did you like the movie?

   Speaker 2: Great.

   The pitch is flat and the word is lengthened even more than a normally stressed word. This intonation pattern shows sarcasm.

As you can see, paying attention to the stress and pitch of a word is very important and can help you with your listening comprehension.

EXERCISE 1

Directions: Listen to the following sentences, and underline the word or phrase with the greatest stress in each sentence.

1. The senator thinks that pollution is decreasing.

2. The senator thinks that pollution is decreasing.

3. The senator thinks that pollution is decreasing.

4. Senator Colwell just completed her second term in office.

5. Senator Colwell just completed her second term in office.

6. Senator Colwell just completed her second term in office.

7. The tax bill did not pass in the House of Representatives.

8. The tax bill did not pass in the House of Representatives.

9. The tax bill did not pass in the House of Representatives.

10. How do you feel about the vice president?

11. How do you feel about the vice president?

12. How do you feel about the vice president?

Directions: *Listen to the following sentences and choose the sentence that best explains the meaning of the stressed word or phrase.*

1.   *a)* It isn't increasing.
    b) It wasn't the president.
    c) It isn't inflation.

2.   *a)* It isn't increasing.
    b) It wasn't the president.
    c) It isn't inflation.

3.   *a)* It isn't increasing.
    b) It wasn't the president.
    c) It isn't inflation.

4.   *a)* She didn't just begin.
    b) It wasn't Dan Schmankie.
    c) It wasn't her first term.

5.   *a)* She didn't just begin.
    b) It wasn't Dan Schmankie.
    c) It wasn't her first term.

6.   *a)* She didn't just begin.
    b) It wasn't Dan Schmankie.
    c) It wasn't her first term.

7.   *a)* I have no special feeling about this information.
    b) I really don't believe this information.
    c) I'm very excited about this information.

8.   *a)* I have no special feeling about this information.
    b) I really don't believe this information.
    c) I'm very excited about this information.

9.   *a)* I have no special feeling about this information.
    b) I really don't believe this information.
    c) I'm very excited about this information

10.   *a)* I can't believe you have such strong feelings about him.
    b) I know your opinion of the president.
    c) You know my opinion. What about yours?

11.   *a)* I can't believe you have such strong feelings about him.
    b) I know your opinion of the president.
    c) You know my opinion. What about yours?

12.   *a)* I can't believe you have such strong feelings about him.
    b) I know your opinion of the president.
    c) You know my opinion. What about yours?

PART FIVE

PRACTICE

EXERCISE 1

Directions: You will hear ten questions. Read the three possible responses and circle the correct answer.

1. *a)* the State of the Union Address
   b) the rising unemployment rate
   c) the three branches of government

2. *a)* The President must be at least 35 years old.
   b) An election is held every four years.
   c) a maximum of two four-year terms

3. *a)* the Supreme Court
   b) the Congress
   c) the President

4. *a)* I want to represent my city.
   b) He doesn't like politics.
   c) The executive branch can veto a bill.

5. *a)* My taxes are too high.
   b) They are revitalizing my neighborhood.
   c) The Governor wants to raise our taxes.

6. *a)* I'm not sure.
   b) They serve for life.
   c) They make the laws.

7. *a)* You should e-mail the President.
   b) You should talk to your senator.
   c) You should go to City Hall.

8. *a)* executive, legislative, judicial
   b) so the power is shared
   c) most state governments have three branches.

9. *a)* none of them
   b) Bella Porter lost the election.
   c) Yes, the election is Tuesday.

10. *a)* It is in the Constitution.
    b) The Congress must vote.
    c) after the President signs it

EXERCISE 2

Directions: You will hear ten sentences. Read the three choices and circle the correct answer.

1. *a)* She thinks education needs improvement.
   b) She wants to spend less on education.
   c) She thinks teachers spend too much money.

2. *a)* Tuyet is worried about health care.
   b) José is worried about homelessness.
   c) Karen is worried about gang violence.

3. a) Florida's population is the same as Illinois'.
   b) The population of Illinois is larger than Hawaii.
   c) The population of Florida is smaller than Hawaii.

4. a) Senators Peterson and Schwartz voted for the bill.
   b) Senators Schwartz and Rodriguez voted for the bill.
   c) Senators Rodriguez and Peterson voted for the bill.

5. a) The Supreme Court will handle the case.
   b) The legislature will handle the case.
   c) The state court will handle the case.

6. a) She is the President.
   b) She is a Congresswoman.
   c) She is a Supreme Court justice.

7. a) They want to punish the homeless.
   b) They don't think homelessness is a problem.
   c) They agree on this issue.

8. a) It is probably winter.
   b) It is probably spring.
   c) It is probably summer.

9. a) Don't you agree that the ideas are bad?
   b) I want to know your opinion.
   c) Your opinion surprises me.

10. a) It is not on Wednesday.
    b) It is not on November 15.
    c) It is not a mayoral election.

EXERCISE 3

Directions: Listen. Each time you hear the bell, circle the sentence that you think is correct.

1. a) The woman is a candidate for governor.
   b) The woman is not a candidate for governor.

2. a) The woman is a candidate for governor.
   b) The woman is not a candidate for governor.

3. a) The speaker is in favor of gun control.
   b) The speaker is not in favor of gun control.

4. a) Taking guns away from citizens is the solution.
   b) Putting people in jail is the solution.

5. a) The speaker is in favor of gun control.
   b) The speaker is not in favor of gun control.

6. a) The speaker is in favor of gun control.
   b) The speaker is not in favor of gun control.
   c) The speaker is in favor of some gun control.

EXERCISE 4

Directions: You will hear two conversations. At the beginning of each conversation, you will hear a question. Listen to the conversation. Then, circle the best answer.

1. *a)* a Town Hall debate
   b) a House of Representatives debate
   c) a Senate debate

2. *a)* his record on the homeless
   b) his record on crime
   c) his record on taxes

EXERCISE 5

Directions: Listen to the sentences. Choose the correct vocabulary word.

1. *a)* revitalize
   b) confined
   c) plummet

2. *a)* sweep it under the rug
   b) limited resources
   c) checks and balances

3. *a)* House of Representatives
   b) Supreme Court
   c) Senate

4. *a)* settler
   b) Constitution
   c) executive

5. *a)* colony
   b) racism
   c) candidate

6. *a)* contentious
   b) advocate
   c) Congress

7. *a)* colonies
   b) unemployment
   c) advocate

8. *a)* cranking out
   b) harassed
   c) skyrocketing

9. *a)* checks and balances
   b) State of the Union
   c) limited resources

10. *a)* sweep it under the rug
    b) checks and balances
    c) cranking out

PART SIX

USING IT: PEOPLE'S GREATEST CONCERNS

For this exercise, you will compare class opinions with those of native English speakers.

Step One: **_Directions:_** Go back to the first exercise in this chapter. As a class, make a tally of the number of students who chose each of the sixteen issues. Make a graph to show which concerns were chosen the most. Did the results surprise you? Why/ why not? Discuss reasons for the concerns chosen.

Step Two: **_Directions:_** Find five native English speakers to interview. Bring the list of sixteen issues, and ask each informant to chose what his or her greatest concern is. Write down the responses and bring them to class.

Step Three: **_Directions:_** You will combine the results from your interviews with the results of your classmates. Use the Tally Sheet to write down the names of your classmates under the column *Student's Name*. Then, write down the five concerns that each classmate got from their interviews. Make sure that you talk to all the students so that your tally sheet is complete. After you have double-checked your tally sheet for accuracy, write your totals in the chart on the Totals chart.

Tally Sheet					
Student's Name	Informant #1's Issue	Informant #2's Issue	Informant #3's Issue	Informant #4's Issue	Informant #5's Issue

Totals		
Issue	Total	Comments

Step Four: *Directions:* In small groups, create a graph to show the results of the interviews. Then, discuss the following questions.

1. Were the concerns that the informants talked about the same ones that you chose as a class? If there were differences, why do you think they exist?

2. Do you think that the types of concerns that native English speakers talk about are the same concerns that people in your native country worry about? Explain.

3. What can we do to make our lives less stressful and eliminate some of our concerns?

CHAPTER SIX

What's Bugging You?

PART ONE

PRE-LISTENING: RADIO SCHEDULE

EXERCISE 1

Using What You Already Know

Directions: In pairs or small groups, look at the KVCH schedule to answer the questions.

KVCH 101.5 FM Schedule

Time	Monday Evening
4:00 4:30	**The Multiple Organic Diner Show** Tonight's topic: Healthy vegetarian recipes for breakfast, lunch, and dinner
5:00 5:30	**News Hour**
6:00 6:30	**Hot Topics** with host Tim Gibson
7:00 7:30	**What's Bugging You?** Call-in relationship advice hosted by Dr. Jennifer E. Wong
8:00	**House Smart** Tips for home improvement with Martha Villa
8:30	**Entertainment News and Reviews** with Mary Liver
9:00 9:30	**Alive! With Larry Queen** Interviews with important people in politics, science, and the arts
10:00 10:30 11:00	**Tunes for the Times** Popular music with DJ Gloria Dylan
11:30 Midnight	**Nite Owl** Call-in show with host Trina Louise

1. How often do you watch TV? How often do you listen to the radio? What are the advantages and disadvantages of each?

2. Do you listen to the radio? If yes, what kinds of programs do you listen to?

3. What kinds of radio programs are the most popular in your home country? Why do you think they are so popular?

4. Which program offered by KVCH interests you the most? Why?

5. Gloria Dylan is the DJ for the show *Tunes for the Times*. What do you think DJ means?

6. What is a call-in show? Which programs listed in the KVCH schedule are call-in shows?

7. What kinds of topics are covered in the program *News Hour*? What specific information would you get if you listened to this program tonight?

8. Look at the description for the *Multiple Organic Diner Show*. What kind of show is this? What are four specific things you might learn from tonight's show (for example, how to make a delicious and nutritious glass of carrot-onion juice)?

9. Look at the description for the show *What's Bugging You?* Make a list of questions that callers might have for Dr. Jennifer E. Wong.

PART TWO

MAIN DIALOGUE

EXERCISE 1

Scanning for the Main Idea/Background Information
Directions: Listen to the dialogue and try to get a general idea of what is happening. Remember, you don't need to understand everything. Just try to think about the following questions:

1. What is the main idea of the dialogue?
2. Where do you think the dialogue is taking place?
3. How many people call the show? Where do you think each person is calling from?
4. Where do you think the speakers live: a big city, a small town, or the country?
5. How do you think each speaker sounds (warm, cold, concerned, angry, and so on)?

EXERCISE 2

Scanning for the Important Points
Directions: Listen to the dialogue again to answer these questions.

1. What kind of show is *What's Bugging You?* Who is Dr. Jenny?

2. What is the first caller's problem?

3. What does Dr. Jenny suggest?

4. What is the second caller's problem?

5. What does Dr. Jenny suggest?

6. What is the third caller's problem?

7. What does Dr. Jenny suggest?

8. Where does Dr. Jenny suggest that all three callers go? Why?

EXERCISE 3

Scanning for Specific Pieces of Information

Directions: Listen to the dialogue one more time and write down as much information as you can about each caller. Don't worry about spelling.

	Name	Age	Job	Married (Yes/No)	Parent (Yes/No)	Person Caller is Worried About	Description of Person Caller is Worried About
Caller 1							
Caller 2							
Caller 3							

EXERCISE 4

Vocabulary in Context

Directions: *Listen to these sentences from the dialogue and circle the answer that has the same meaning.*

1. *a)* She was drunk.
    b) She was lazy.

2. *a)* She didn't want to study for the test.
    b) She didn't want to take the test.

3. *a)* She doesn't care about her classes.
    b) She doesn't tell me what she's doing.

4. *a)* You are too strict with her.
    b) You think something is 100 percent true before you really know.

5. *a)* Let's look at the facts clearly.
    b) Let's look at the history of the situation.

6. *a)* She will talk freely with you.
    b) She will have a good time.

7. *a)* My wife is planning a party.
    b) My wife is cheating.

8. *a)* You must share equally.
    b) You must fight for your rights.

9. *a)* frightening
    b) pleasant

10. *a)* understanding and kind
    b) cold and distant

EXERCISE 5

Directions: *In pairs or small groups, discuss the following questions. Then, as a class, compare your answers.*

1. Do you agree with Dr. Jenny's advice for each caller? If not, what advice would you give the caller(s)?

2. Who do you go to for advice about problems in your life? Why do you go to that person?

3. Have you ever called a radio or TV show to ask for advice or to comment on some part of the show? If yes, explain. If no, do you think you would ever call one of these programs? Explain.

4. Have you ever written a letter to a newspaper or a radio or TV show? If yes, tell your group about the letter and any response you may have received. If no, can you think of a show or newspaper that you would like to write a letter to? Explain.

5. Which of the major media (newspapers, TV, radio, the Internet) do you prefer for getting news? Explain.

Oral Journal Homework Assignment

Directions: *Prepare a short talk about a current event that you are very interested in and have strong feelings about. Choose a story from the newspaper, radio, TV, or Internet. It can be an international, national, or local story. In your speech, you will talk about the story and then give your opinion about it. Use this rough outline to help you organize your speech.*

I. Introduction
   A. Where you found the story
   B. Why you chose this story
   C. Story summary
      1. The facts of the story
         a)
         b)
         c)
         d)
      2. What experts say
         a)
         b)
         c)
   D. Your opinion

II. Your Editorial
   A. Reasons for your opinion
      1.
      2.
      3.
      4.
      5.
   B. Who agrees with you
      1.
      2.
      3.
   C. What should be done (if you are opposed to the issue/situation)
         or
      How the issue/situation is good for people (if you agree)
      1.
      2.
      3.
      4.

IV. Conclusion
   A. Summary of issue
   B. Why the class should agree with your opinion

PART THREE

EXPANSION

The Newspaper

EXERCISE 1

Directions: In pairs or small groups, decide in which section of a newspaper you would find the following headlines. Then, as a class, compare your answers.

Headline	Newspaper Section(s)
Goniff International to Hire 5,000 New Workers	
S and G Supermarket Opens New Store on Third Street	
North High School *Kettsels* Win Basketball Finals	
U. S. Congress Overrides President's Veto	
Attack of the Flying Monkeys is Number One Film in Asia	
Danny Martino and Stella Padudi Arrested near Chicago	
Major Hurricane Destroys Hospital in Miami, Florida	
Supreme Court Ruling on Monaghan Case Expected Tomorrow	
Drunk Driver Kills Teenager Near Mall	
Great Condition Used Cars On Sale This Week Only	
Cheap and Easy Soup Recipes	

EXERCISE 2

Directions: *Listen to the following lecture about newspapers. Each time you hear the bell, write down the main point that has been discussed.*

1. _____

2. _____

3. _____

4. _____

5. _____

6. _____

7. _____

8. _____

EXERCISE 3

Directions: *Listen to the lecture again. Each time you hear the bell, answer the question for the section of the lecture you have just heard.*

1. What is *freedom of the press*?

2. What is the difference between *national* and *local* newspapers?

3. How do newspaper publishers make money?

4. Why do most front-page stories continue somewhere inside the front section?

5. Where is the most important information in a news article?

6. What is the difference between a *straight* news story and an *opinion* or *editorial*?

7. Besides news, what do newspapers include?

8. What is important about newspapers in the United States?

EXERCISE 4

Directions: Listen to the lecture one more time. Use the following rough outline to take notes. Add any numbers or letters that you feel may be necessary. After you have taken notes, get in small groups to create a detailed outline of the lecture. Make sure to follow proper outline form. When you are finished, write your outline on the chalkboard. Compare outlines. As a class, critique each outline. Which outline is the best? Why?

The Daily Newspaper

I. Introduction
    A. Background information
        1. _____
        2. Papers around for long time
    B. Freedom of the Press
        1. _____
            a) negative and critical stories protected
    C. Important way to get information
            a) _____
            b) papers cheap/easy

II. Overview of American Newspapers
    A. Background information
        1. _____
        2. _____
    B. _____
        1. _____
            a) Available everywhere
            b) _____
                i) Wall St. Journal
                ii) _____
        2. Local newspapers
            a) For cities/areas
            b) Examples
                i) _____
                ii) _____

III. Newspaper Business
    A. Advertising
        1. Papers get money from ads
        2. _____
        3. Newspapers are cheap because of ads

IV. Front Page
    A. Purpose: _____
    B. Kinds of stories
        1. _____
        2. _____
        3. _____
    C. Headline stories continue:
        1. _____
        2. publishers want people to buy papers

V. Good news articles
    A. Lead paragraph
        1. WH–questions: _____
        2. saves time for busy readers
        3. rest of article: _____

VI. Straight and Opinion/Editorial News
    A. Straight news
        1. _____
        2. _____
        3. readers decide for themselves
    B. _____
        1. opinions/feelings
            a) current news story
            b) political candidate
        2. letters to the editor

VII. Newspaper Sections
    A. World, national, and local news
    B. Other parts
        1. _____
        2. _____
        3. _____
        4. _____
        5. _____
    C. Finding a section

VIII. Conclusion:
    _____

EXERCISE 5

Directions: In pairs or small groups, discuss the following questions. Then, as a class, compare your answers.

1. How many local daily newspapers are available where you live? What are their names?

2. Do you think freedom of the press is a good American law? Explain.

3. What section of the newspaper do you think is the most important? Why? Which section is your favorite? Why?

4. Do you feel that newspapers give you enough information about current events? Do newspapers cover the kind of stories you are interested in? Explain.

5. American journalists are not allowed to offer their opinion in a straight news story. Do you think this is a good idea? Explain.

6. Do you read a newspaper regularly? If yes, what is the name of the paper and what language is it printed in?

7. How are newspapers in the U.S.A. similar to newspapers in your native country? How are they different?

PART FOUR

FOCUS: TAG QUESTIONS

The structure of a sentence in English can sometimes be confusing for you if it is different from your native language. One example of this is negative yes/no questions. You know that a negative yes/no question does *not* have a negative meaning: it simply is a way for speakers to show listeners that they are almost sure that the statement is true and that they are just checking to be 100% certain.

Example: Ted, *didn't* you say you were studying astrophysics?
(The speaker believes that Ted is studying astrophysics. She just wants to be 100% sure.)

English uses **tag questions** in the same way that it uses negative yes/no questions.

Example: Ted, you said that you were studying astrophysics, *didn't you?*
(Again, the speaker believes that Ted is studying astrophysics. She just wants to be 100% sure.)

Tag questions can be affirmative or negative depending on the meaning of the sentence.

When the speaker believes that the information is true, an affirmative statement is used, followed by a negative tag.

Example: Chez Latidaz serves romantic dinners, *doesn't it?*
(The speaker believes that Chez Latidaz serves romantic dinners. He just wants to be 100% sure.)

When the speaker believes that information is not true, a negative statement is used, followed by an affirmative tag.

Example: You don't have any proof that your daughter was drinking, *do you*, Denise?
(The speaker believes that Denise does not have any proof. She just wants to be 100% sure.)

It is important to remember that the tags in tag questions are not really affirmative or negative. The main statements indicate if the information is affirmative or negative.

Tag Question Review

Remember, tags are always auxiliaries: *be*, *have*, modals (*can, could, might, should, would,* etc.), or, for all other verbs: *do.*

Examples:

Statement	Tag
Negative *Be*	Affirmative *Be*
You **aren't** sure about her drinking,	**are** you?
Affirmative *Have*	Negative *Have*
You **'ve** talked to your daughter about that,	**haven't** you?
Affirmative *Can*	Negative Modal *Can*
You **can** find the time to talk to her,	**can't** you?
Affirmative *Verb*	Negative *Do*
You **know** that wonderful little restaurant Chez Latidaz,	**don't** you?

Knowing the difference between affirmative yes/no questions, negative yes/no questions, and affirmative and negative tag questions is very important if you want to develop good listening attack strategies. Without this information, you might give incorrect answers to everyday questions. Your knowledge of these forms will help you to be a better listener and a more accurate speaker.

EXERCISE 1

Directions: Listen to each statement. Then choose the correct tag for each one.

Example:
a) did she?
b) didn't she?
c) hasn't she?
d) has she?

1.
a) doesn't it?
b) does it?
c) isn't it
d) is it?

2.
a) do they?
b) don't they?
c) does it?
d) doesn't it?

3.
a) could you?
b) can't you?
c) couldn't you?
d) can you?

4.
a) isn't it?
b) is it?
c) does it?
d) doesn't it?

5. *a)* hadn't you?
    b) had you?
    c) shouldn't you?
    d) should you?

6. *a)* haven't they?
    b) don't they?
    c) have they?
    d) do they?

7. *a)* don't they?
    b) won't they
    c) do they?
    d) will they?

8. *a)* don't they?
    b) do they?
    c) haven't they?
    d) have they?

9. *a)* don't you?
    b) won't you?
    c) wouldn't you?
    d) would you?

10. *a)* don't they?
    b) do they?
    c) aren't they?
    d) are they?

EXERCISE 2

Directions: Listen to the sentences. Then, choose the sentence that has the same meaning as the sentence you hear. Circle the correct letter.

Example:
    a) I think it has the largest circulation.
    b) I want to know if it has the largest circulation.
    c) I think it doesn't have the largest circulation.

1. *a)* I think you need to worry about the truth.
    b) I want to know if you need to worry about the truth.
    c) I think you don't have to worry about the truth.

2. *a)* I think there are ads in the paper.
    b) I want to know if there are ads in the paper.
    c) I think there aren't ads in the paper.

3. *a)* I think you can get advice.
    b) I want to know if you can get advice.
    c) I think you can't get advice.

4. *a)* I think they are controversial.
    b) I want to know if they are controversial.
    c) I think they aren't controversial.

5. *a)* I think they ran that article.
    b) I want to know if they ran that article.
    c) I think they didn't run that article.

6. *a)* I think there are more national newspapers.
    b) I want to know if there are more national newspapers.
    c) I think there are not more national newspapers.

7. *a)* I think that is the time.
    b) I want to know if that is the time.
    c) I think that isn't the time.

8. *a)* I think it is online.
    b) I want to know if it is online.
    c) I think it isn't online.

9. *a)* I think they always have commercials.
    b) I want to know if they always have commercials.
    c) I think they don't always have commercials.

10. *a)* I think newspapers can deliver as quickly.
    b) I want to know if newspapers can deliver as quickly.
    c) I think newspapers can't deliver as quickly.

EXERCISE 3

Directions: With a partner, write at least ten yes/no questions about current events in the news. Make sure that everyone in the class knows the answers to the questions. Try to vary your questions so that you have several affirmative yes/no questions, several negative yes/no questions, several affirmative tag questions, and several negative questions.

Examples: Wasn't the weather unusually hot yesterday?
Did (name of sports team) win yesterday's game?
The big story in the news today is (give name), isn't it?
You can't get radio news 24 hours a day, can you?

When you have finished, find new partners. Practice asking and answering each other's questions.

PART FIVE

PRACTICE

EXERCISE **1**

Directions: *You will hear ten questions. Read the three possible responses and choose the correct answer.*

1. ***a)*** I got an *A* on my research paper.
   b) This book is really interesting.
   c) My car broke down again.

2. ***a)*** Yes, I like to read the newspaper.
   b) at least once a week
   c) The *Miami Herald* is my favorite newspaper.

3. ***a)*** aren't they?
   b) haven't they?
   c) don't they?

4. ***a)*** *Attack of the Flying Monkeys* is a violent flick.
   b) I'm not sure. Check the index.
   c) You should read the lead paragraph.

5. ***a)*** There are too many ads in the newspaper.
   b) My local newspaper costs 75 cents.
   c) Stores and companies cover most of the cost.

6. ***a)*** Yes, I understood the question.
   b) I was really hungry.
   c) I hadn't studied.

7. ***a)*** a reporter
   b) an editor
   c) an advertiser

8. ***a)*** That's one of my favorite shows.
   b) right before *Tunes for Our Times*
   c) It's a 30-minute interview show.

9. ***a)*** Yes, I didn't.
   b) No, I did.
   c) Yes, I did.

10. ***a)*** *The Wall Street Journal*
    b) *USA Today*
    c) *The Los Angeles Times*

EXERCISE **2**

Directions: *You will hear ten sentences. Read the three choices and circle the correct answer.*

1. ***a)*** *USA Today* is less popular than *The Wall Street Journal.*
   b) *The New York Times* is more popular than *USA Today.*
   c) *The Wall Street Journal* isn't as popular as the *New York Times.*

2. ***a)*** Alexander really likes Dr. Jenny's radio program.
   b) Alexander never calls Dr. Jenny's radio program.
   c) Alexander often disagrees with Dr. Jenny's advice.

3. *a)* It is a very strange and confusing idea.
   b) It is something the government can't take away.
   c) It is only for certain special citizens.

4. *a)* More people read the newspaper than watch TV.
   b) Twenty-five percent of Americans don't read the newspaper.
   c) Everyone who owns a TV reads the newspaper.

5. *a)* Senator Shmankie will be arrested.
   b) Senator Shmankie is probably married.
   c) Senator Shmankie is from New Jersey.

6. *a)* I think the show can give you relationship advice.
   b) I think the show can't give you relationship advice.
   c) I want to know if the show can give you relationship advice.

7. *a)* The program tells me what's happening in other countries.
   b) The program tells me what's happening in my community.
   c) The program tells me what's happening in other states.

8. *a)* I read the newspaper.
   b) I watched TV.
   c) I listened to the radio.

9. *a)* I like the band Wheezie better.
   b) I like the band Back Alley Boys better.
   c) I like both bands the same.

10. *a)* I'm pretty sure I've seen the name *The Times* a lot.
    b) I don't think *The Times* is a popular name, but I want to be sure.
    c) Someone told me that *The Times* is a popular name, but I really don't know.

EXERCISE 3

Directions: *Listen to the conversation. Each time you hear the bell, circle the sentence that you think is correct.*

1. *a)* This is a violent news story.
   b) This isn't a violent news story.

2. *a)* This is a violent news story.
   b) This isn't a violent news story.

3. *a)* The Kandizaen team easily won the game.
   b) The Kandizaen team had difficulty winning the game.

4. *a)* The Kandizaen team had difficulty winning the game.
   b) The Kandizaen team easily won the game.

5. *a)* This is mostly an editorial.
   b) This is mostly a news story.

6. *a)* This is mostly a news story.
   b) This is mostly an editorial.

EXERCISE 4

Directions: *You will hear three conversations. At the beginning of each conversation, you will hear a question. Listen to the conversation. Then, circle the best answer.*

1. *a)* the business section
    b) the sports section
    c) the local news section

2. *a)* international
    b) national
    c) local

3. *a)* She listens to the show every day.
    b) She wants to give Dr. Jenny some advice.
    c) She thinks Dr. Jenny's advice is really good.

EXERCISE 5

Directions: *Listen to the sentence. Choose the correct vocabulary word.*

1. *a)* editorial
    b) lead paragraph
    c) intimidating

2. *a)* half as cool as you
    b) lethargic
    c) clam up

3. *a)* editorial
    b) ditch
    c) open up

4. *a)* what's bugging you
    b) jumping the gun
    c) half as cool as you

5. *a)* compromise
    b) intimidating
    c) lethargic

6. *a)* intimidating
    b) rocket scientist
    c) ditch

7. *a)* world news
    b) national news
    c) local news

8. *a)* I've been working a lot of overtime.
    b) I exercise regularly and eat healthy food.
    c) I got a good night's sleep last night.

9. *a)* front page
    b) lead paragraph
    c) editorial

10. *a)* headline
    b) opinion
    c) compromise

PART SIX

USING IT: MAKING NEWS

Directions:

For this exercise, the class will produce a news broadcast. First, as a class, decide on a name for your show and the kinds of stories you will include. Then, form groups to work on the broadcast. Each group will be responsible for one portion of the show: the international news, the national news, the local news, the entertainment news, the weather report, the sports news, the editorial, and so on. After you've written and practiced your stories in your groups, choose one member of your group to be the reporter for the broadcast.

You will need to select two students to act as *anchors* (people who introduce the reporters on radio or TV) for the broadcast. While each group is working on its stories, the anchors should visit each group to find out what stories will be reported. The anchors should then decide the order of the stories. When everyone is ready, the broadcast will begin.

If you are an anchor, you will begin by introducing the broadcast (introduce yourself, the date, the program, and so on). Maybe give an overview of the leading headlines that will be reported in the show. You will then introduce each story. Remember to use smooth transitions between each report. For example, *we now move from national news to a story of local interest.* Also, remember to introduce the reporter(s) of each story. Finally, after the broadcast is completed, think of a way to end the broadcast.

If you are a reporter, reviewer, weatherperson, or other broadcaster, remember to introduce your story and to give all of the most important information: *who, what, when, where, how,* and *why.* Make sure that you use appropriate transitions to send the broadcast back to the anchors.

After you have finished your broadcast, vote to see who deserves the award for best journalist. Once you have decided, give reasons for why this person was best.

CHAPTER SEVEN

I've Got Your Number!

PART ONE

PRE-LISTENING: BUYER BEWARE

Using What You Already Know

Directions: In pairs or small groups, read the information in the boxes to answer the questions.

legitimate
Fair, according to the law

scam
A trick or dishonest plan to try and get your money

A *consumer* is a person who buys a product or service. To be a smart consumer, you need to know when a business offer is **legitimate**, and when it is a **scam**. There are many methods that businesses use to make offers including mail offers, telephone solicitations, and TV, radio, and print-ad offers. It is important to be able to recognize when an offer is a scam. Here is a list of some common consumer scams and how you can avoid them:

🕮 In Your Mailbox

Mail that you did not ask to receive is called *junk mail*. While most junk mail contains legitimate ads, some are trying to scam you.

Travel/Vacation Scam:

The Pitch: You receive a postcard telling you that you have won a *free* cruise or vacation package. All you have to do is call a phone number and/or pay a fee to get your prize.

The Scam: The prize is not free because you have to pay a fee or call a special phone number that is a 900-number that charges $2.00 a minute.

The Solution: Throw the postcard away and save your money for a real vacation.

☎ On Your Telephone

When companies advertise by phone, it's called *telemarketing.* Most telemarketers are legitimate, but some are trying to scam you.

Credit Card Scam:

The Pitch: A friendly person tells you that they are calling from your credit card company and that you were overcharged on something you recently bought with your credit card. All you have to do is give the person your credit card number and the money will be refunded to your account.

The Scam: The person calling you was not from the credit card company, and has just stolen your credit card number!

The Solution: Do not give out your credit card number or other personal information to a telemarketer.

◎ In The Store

Scams do not only happen on the telephone and in the mail. They can happen in a store.

The Bait and Switch Scam:

The Pitch: You see an ad in the newspaper for a $500.00 chair that is on sale for only $150.00! This is *exactly* the chair you want, so you go to the store and ask to see it. The salesperson tells you that all the $150.00 chairs have been sold and then tries to sell you a different chair that costs $300.00

The Scam: The store probably never had any $150.00 chairs, but used the advertisement to get you really interested (the *bait*) so that you would come into the store. Once inside the store, the salesperson tried to get you to buy a different chair (the *switch*).

The Solution: If the salesperson doesn't have the sale chair that was advertised, leave the store and go somewhere else to buy it.

1. What do you think *consumer awareness* is?

2. What's the difference between a legitimate offer and a scam?

3. As used in the scam descriptions, what do you think *pitch* means?

4. How often do you receive junk mail? Do you ever read it? Explain.

5. What is a *telemarketer*? Has a telemarketer ever called you? If yes, what did you do?

6. Is there any situation when it's okay to give your credit card number or other information to a business over the phone? Describe.

7. What is the difference between an 800 phone number and a 900 phone number? Have you ever called a 900 phone number? Explain.

8. What do you think *Buyer Beware* means?

PART TWO

MAIN DIALOGUE

Scanning for the Main Idea/Background Information

Directions: Listen to the selection and try to get a general idea of what is happening. Remember, you don't have to understand everything. Just try to think about the following questions:

1. What is the main idea of the dialogue?
2. Where do you think the dialogue is taking place?
3. What is the relationship between the speakers?
4. How old do you think the speakers are?
5. How do you think each speaker sounds (warm, cold, concerned, angry, and so on)?

Scanning for the Important Points

Directions: Now, listen to the dialogue again to answer these questions:

1. What is the general topic of conversation during this dialogue?

2. Who is the first person to call?

3. How does Debra end the conversation?

4. Who is the second caller?

5. How does Jake end the conversation?

6. Who is the third caller?

7. How does Owen end the call?

Scanning for Specific Pieces of Information

Directions: Listen to the dialogue one more time and fill in the chart with information about the three telephone calls.

Caller	Name	Company	Offer	Price	Conditions and/or Special Features
1.					
2.					
3.					

EXERCISE 4

Vocabulary in Context

Directions: Listen to these sentences from the dialogue and circle the answer that has the same meaning.

1. *a)* I'm tired.
   b) I'm hungry.

2. *a)* Mr. Carson is the boss.
   b) Mr. Carson is funny looking.

3. *a)* You can call any time you want.
   b) You can call as often as you want.

4. *a)* This is a fair deal.
   b) This is a cheap deal.

5. *a)* a lawyer
   b) a salesperson

6. *a)* They really bother me.
   b) They have a difficult job.

7. *a)* You will have to pay for the room.
   b) You will not have to pay for the room.

8. *a)* A machine is calling.
   b) A person is calling.

9. *a)* frightening
   b) disturbing

10. *a)* a bad idea
    b) a smart idea

EXERCISE 5

Directions: In pairs or small groups, discuss the following questions. Then, as a class, compare your answers.

1. Is junk mail common in your native country? If yes, how is it similar to/different from junk mail in the U.S.A.? If no, what other ways do people get information?

2. Have you ever received a letter saying that you've won a prize? If yes, what did you do?

3. Have you, or someone you know, ever been the victim of a scam? Describe the scam and what the person did to solve the problem.

4. In the main dialogue, Owen asked the telemarketer for his home phone number. Was that a good strategy in this situation? Explain.

5. What other strategies can you use to stop telemarketers from bothering you at home?

Oral Journal Homework Assignment

Directions: Prepare a short speech in which you discuss your feelings about advertising.

Here are some things you may want to think about in organizing your speech:
Do you think there is too much advertising? Not enough advertising? Should advertising be in newspapers, on TV and radio, and on billboards, or should the places advertising is allowed be limited? What's good about advertising? What's bad about advertising? Does advertising work? If yes, what kind of advertising works best? Does advertising influence the purchases that you make?

In organizing your speech, first decide what major point you want to make about advertising. (For example: *Advertising is beneficial to consumers,* or *There are many problems with adverting today.*) Then, make sure you include strong examples to support the position you take on that issue. Finally, conclude your speech with a few statements that convince the audience of your position.

To prepare your speech, you may use the rough outline that follows.

I. Introduction
   A. General statement about advertising
   B. Your position about advertising

II. Problems with advertising/Benefits of advertising
   A. Problem/Benefit
      1. example
         a) detail
         b) detail
      2. example
         a) detail
   B. Problem/Benefit
      1. example
      2. a) detail
         b) detail
         c) detail
   C. Problem/Benefit
      1. example
         a) detail
      2. example
         a) detail
      3. example
         a) detail
         b) detail
III. Conclusion
   A. Summary of your position
   B. How/why the audience should care about this topic

Note that the sample outline is only for a speech in which you are either completely in favor of the various kinds of advertising or completely against them. If some forms are acceptable to you and others are not, you will need to change the outline. If you chose another position, you will need to change the outline. With your instructor, discuss changes you will need to make for your speech.

PART THREE

EXPANSION

persuasion
Make someone believe or
feel sure about something

Propaganda

Directions: *Read and discuss the following information with your instructor. Then in pairs or small groups answer the questions that follow.*

In the United States, citizens have many freedoms and choices. They can get information from a free press, can make their own decisions about which political candidates to vote for, and are free to shop for many different kinds of goods and services. Having freedom means making many choices, and an important skill to use to make responsible decisions is called *critical thinking*. Critical thinking is making a decision only after carefully studying and understanding *all* sides of an issue. Critical thinkers look at all the facts, examples, statistics, causes and effects, and details carefully. They look to see which information is correct and which information is misleading or perhaps even wrong.

People using critical thinking always think for themselves and try to use sound logic to arrive at reasonable assumptions. For example, a person using critical thinking when buying a car will try to get as much information as possible about the cars she is interested in before spending any money. She will not just listen to one salesperson tell her about one car or believe that something about that car is true simply because the salesperson says it is. She will be sure to talk to many different people and read as much information as possible about all of the cars before making a final decision.

Because businesses want people to buy their products, they try to influence them through the use of **persuasion.** Sometimes advertisers use false information or other tricks to persuade people to buy their products or to use their services. When businesses use unclear facts, emotions, or unsupported opinions to try and persuade others, it is called *propaganda.*

Good critical thinkers are able to recognize propaganda and not let it affect their decisions. For example, if a car salesperson tells you that you should buy his car because it's the same car that the President of the United States drives, you should know that this is propaganda and not useful information. Critical thinking is an important skill to use in everyday life because it helps you to recognize when propaganda is being used. Following is a list of seven propaganda devices (strategies) that are frequently used to try and change your opinions.

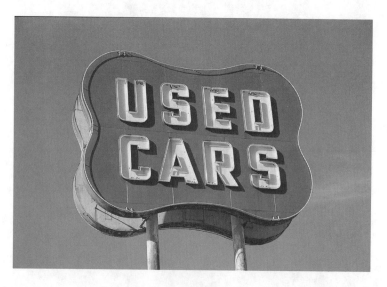

Seven Basic Propaganda Devices*

Propaganda Strategy	Example
1. **Name-Calling** Making a personal attack against a person, product, or idea without any proof. Using words that people commonly think of as bad or negative to persuade.	In an ad for a shoe company, you are told that another company's shoes are not as good because they are old-fashioned and ugly.
2. **Glittering Generalities** Making a person, product, or idea sound really wonderful without any proof. Using good or positive words to persuade you (This is the opposite of *Name-Calling*).	In a commercial for a car, you are told that the car is the latest, most modern car and that its design uses the most advanced technology available today.
3. **Transfer** Using a respected authority figure (church, government, professional organization) or a symbol (a flag or cross) to persuade you. The respect of the figure or symbols transfers to what is being sold.	In an ad for aspirin, an actor playing a doctor tells you that the medicine will work great. You think the aspirin must be good because a *doctor* is talking about it.
4. **Testimonial** Using a famous person (actor, singer, sports star) to persuade you.	An Olympic athlete's picture is placed on a cereal box. You think that eating this cereal will make you an Olympic champion, too.
5. **Plain Folks** Making a person or product sound good by saying that the people involved are not rich or different but are just like everybody else, so that people will trust the person or product.	In an ad for a fast-food restaurant, the president of the company wears casual clothes and sits in a small house. We think he is just like us, so we trust him and want to buy his hamburgers.
6. **Card Stacking** (Fear) Trying to trick people by showing only one very negative side of a competing product, candidate, or issue to make people afraid of the competition.	In an ad for telephone service, you are told that the competition has recently raised its rates and that it is known for having poor customer service. You are told nothing about the rate raises or about the customer service record of the advertising company.
7. **Bandwagon** Making a person or product sound good by saying that it is the one that most people like. Persuading you to join in so you are not different from everyone else.	In a commercial for soap, you are told that 99% of the people like this soap better than any other. You want to be like everybody else, so you buy this brand of soap, too.

*From The Institute for Propaganda Analysis

1. What is critical thinking? What do you need to do in order to be a successful critical thinker?

2. What is persuasion?

3. What is propaganda?

4. Who often uses propaganda? Why do they use it?

5. How many of the basic propaganda devices have you seen used? Describe.

6. Which of the basic propaganda devices do you think is the most effective? Explain.

7. Have you ever bought a product because the advertisement persuaded you? Did you buy it after using critical thinking or because you were a victim of propaganda?

8. Is propaganda used in your native country? Explain.

We can see that propaganda is widely used in advertising to persuade you to buy products or services. Propaganda is also commonly used by politicians, governments, and other organizations to try and persuade you to accept their views, to vote for their candidates, or to take certain actions. If you do not use critical thinking in these situations, the results can be very dangerous. For example, if you vote without using critical thinking, people might get elected who do not really share your ideas or represent you. The actions that they take could be very harmful to you or to your community. In order to make thoughtful and logical choices about information that you are presented with in *all* situations, it is important to learn how to recognize propaganda in its many contexts.

EXERCISE 2

Directions: *In pairs or small groups, read the following descriptions, which make use of propaganda. For each one, decide which propaganda device is used.*

1. In the 1970s, President Jimmy Carter often visited the homes of average American families throughout the United States in order to learn how they felt about major issues of concern. He would stay at these homes overnight, during which time the media would show him eating meals with these normal, everyday citizens.

2. (From a speech delivered in the U.S. Senate)
Senator Swifty's bill is a good bill because it was written by a true American who has served his country well and is a decent and honest man. This bill was written by the same man who created the Teenage Outreach program in 1997. He is an intelligent and creative thinker who understands what America really needs.

3. A television commercial features a group of people who are all drinking the same soft drink. A sad-looking young boy enters the scene. Someone offers him a can of the soft drink. He takes a sip and breaks out into a big smile. All of the other people wink at the boy to show him that he has made a smart decision and that he can now join in the fun.

4. (From a commercial for toothpaste)

Teresa: David, are you still using *Bleem,* that tired old toothpaste my grandmother used to buy? That's what the geriatric generation uses. You don't want to feel like an old fogey, do you?

David: Well no, I guess not.

Teresa: You need to start brushing with *Sentadent,* the toothpaste for the young at heart. Take my advice and try *Sentadent,* you'll be glad you did!

5. (From a letter by a famous actor sent to voters)

Jen Mont-O'Han is a close and personal friend of mine and I would like to ask you to vote for her. I have known Ms. Mont-O'Han for over ten years and consider her one of the warmest and kindest women I know. If you have enjoyed watching me on TV over the years, I'd like you to show me how much by helping to reelect this highly experienced and trustworthy member of the state senate.

Yours truly,

Tony Bill Ohney

6. (From a speech at a political rally. The candidate is waving a flag and wearing his old army hat)

Good afternoon. I am here today as a former member of the military who is proud to be an American. I am extremely pleased to announce to you that our local Veterans' organization has decided to stand by me in this election. I think you'll agree that if I am good enough for these true heroes of our country, I am good enough for you.

7. (From an editorial about bilingual education)

People who are against bilingual education are quite simply racists who are intolerant of people of diverse backgrounds. They are afraid of cultural differences and, instead of embracing those differences, they attack them. Good citizens should condemn the opponents of bilingual education in order to send a clear message that diversity is good for our nation.

EXERCISE 3

Directions: Listen to the following commercials and speeches. For each one, circle the propaganda strategy used.

1. *a)* Card Stacking (Fear)
     b) Testimonial
     c) Name-Calling
     d) Glittering Generalities

2. *a)* Plain Folks
     b) Testimonial
     c) Glittering Generalities
     d) Card Stacking (Fear)

3. *a)* Testimonial
   b) Name-Calling
   c) Transfer
   d) Bandwagon

4. *a)* Card Stacking (Fear)
   b) Name-Calling
   c) Glittering Generalities
   d) Plain Folks

5. *a)* Bandwagon
   b) Transfer
   c) Testimonial
   d) Plain Folks

6. *a)* Glittering Generalities
   b) Testimonial
   c) Bandwagon
   d) Transfer

7. *a)* Bandwagon
   b) Plain Folks
   c) Name-Calling
   d) Testimonial

8. *a)* Testimonial
   b) Transfer
   c) Glittering Generalities
   d) Plain Folks

PART FOUR

FOCUS: ACTIVE AND PASSIVE FORMS

Section 1 Active and Passive Verbs

You have already studied active and passive verb forms in English. For example, you know that if you hear the active sentence, *the Patlantic Telephone Company called Debra last night during dinner,* the Patlantic Telephone company did the action (calling Debra) and Debra received the action (getting the call).

You also know that if you hear the passive sentence, *Debra was called by the Patlantic Telephone Company last night during dinner,* the Patlantic Telephone Company still did the action and Debra still received the action.

In active sentences, the subject of the sentence is the doer of the action.

In passive sentences, the subject is the receiver or object of the doer's action.

To become better listeners, you need to be able to recognize a passive sentence. Passive sentences are signaled by:

BE   + PAST PARTICIPLE + (by+ the real doer of the action)

Passive sentences only sometimes end with *by* followed by the doer of the action.

Example: Mr. Johnson's free trip to Hawaii was paid for by his credit card company.

Here it is important to say who paid for the trip.
If the doer is not important or is unknown, then *by* is not used.

Example: Unfortunately, propaganda is commonly used.

Here, there is no specific person to name, so *by* + *doer* is not necessary.

EXERCISE 1

Directions: *Listen to the following sentences. For each sentence, circle the correct form of the verb that you hear.*

1. Active   Passive
2. Active   Passive
3. Active   Passive
4. Active   Passive
5. Active   Passive
6. Active   Passive
7. Active   Passive
8. Active   Passive

EXERCISE 2

Directions: *Listen to the following sentences. For each sentence that you hear, decide who the* doer *of the action is. Circle the correct answer.*

1. *a)* Nancy
   b) the credit card company

2. *a)* my teacher
   b) me

3. *a)* Lisa
   b) We don't know.

4. *a)* the telephone company
   b) Kitty

5. *a)* the university
   b) We don't know.

6. *a)* Mr. Lopez
   b) Louisa

7. *a)* decision makers
   b) critical thinking

8. *a)* the device
   b) most politicians

Section 2 Active and Passive Adjectives

Many adjectives come from verbs and are either active or passive. Let's review how active and passive adjectives are made.

Doer versus Receiver

Active Adjectives for the Doer

Active adjectives describe the doer of the action.

Example: The credit card offer confused Jill.
The credit card was *confusing*.
It was a *confusing* offer.

Here, *the credit card offer* did something: it confused. If we want to describe *the offer* and its action, we use *confusing:* the active (present participle *–ing)* adjective.

Passive Adjectives for the Receiver

Passive adjectives describe the receiver of an action.

Example: Jill was confused by the credit card offer.
Jill was *confused*.
Jill was a *confused* consumer.

Here, Jill received something: she received confusion. If we want to describe Jill and what she received, we use *confused:* the passive (past participle *–ed)* adjective.

Continuing versus Completed Action

Active Adjectives for Continuing Action

Active adjectives (present participles) can also show that an action is still taking place.

Example: The child ran in front of the *stopping* car.
(The car was still moving when the child ran in front of it.)

Passive Adjectives for Completed Action

Passive Adjectives (past participles) can also show that an action has been completed.

Example: The child ran in front of the *stopped* car.
(The car was no longer moving when the child ran in front of it.)

EXERCISE 3

Directions: *Listen to the following sentences and circle the sentence with the same meaning.*

Example: ⓐ Rodney didn't understand.
              b) The teacher didn't understand.

1.   a)   The students were annoyed.
    b)   The students were annoying.

2.   a)   Martha was embarrassed.
    b)   Martha was embarrassing.

3.   a)   Theresa's grade was disappointing.
    b)   Theresa's grade was disappointed.

4.   a)   The students are bored.
    b)   The students are boring.

5.   a)   Sandy was shocking.
    b)   Sandy was shocked.

EXERCISE 4

Directions: *Listen to the following sentences. Then, circle the sentence with the same meaning.*

Example: a)   The teacher didn't understand.
              ⓑ The students didn't understand.

1.   a)   My neighbor scares me.
    b)   My neighbor is scared.

2.   a)   Donna thinks she likes him.
    b)   Donna thinks he likes her.

3.   a)   The books were in the air.
    b)   The books were on the floor.

4.   a)   Their son is still a child.
    b)   Their son is an adult.

5.   a)   They are still married.
    b)   They are not married.

PART FIVE

PRACTICE

EXERCISE **1**

Directions: You will hear ten questions. Read the three possible responses and choose the correct answer.

1. *a)* only when you are afraid of being cheated
   b) when you want to persuade someone
   c) all of the time

2. *a)* The shopper didn't buy a CD player.
   b) The store was having a sale.
   c) The salesperson was rude.

3. *a)* She tried to, but I wasn't convinced.
   b) She is a very dishonest person.
   c) Yes, she wants to buy a car.

4. *a)* I don't answer when I'm eating dinner.
   b) I thought the call was a scam.
   c) I stopped counting after three.

5. *a)* I haven't taken a vacation in three years.
   b) Talk to the head honcho.
   c) They offer free vacations all of the time.

6. *a)* The telemarketer was convinced.
   b) I was convincing.
   c) The telemarketer was convincing.

7. *a)* Read your junk mail.
   b) Ask a telemarketer.
   c) the Bureau for Consumer Fraud

8. *a)* One is an advertisement.
   b) They both contain propaganda.
   c) This one is from a legitimate business.

9. *a)* Vicky told him that the car was in perfect condition.
   b) He told Vicky that the car had only 1000 miles on it.
   c) Vicky is a very smart consumer.

10. *a)* using all negative words to describe something
    b) I'm not sure. Let's ask the teacher.
    c) when a respected authority is used

EXERCISE **2**

Directions: You will hear ten sentences. Read the three choices and circle the correct answer.

1. *a)* Jeffrey never looks at ads.
   b) Jeffrey uses critical thinking.
   c) Jeffrey only watches TV.

2. *a)* Javier agreed with Kate.
   b) Javier paid for lunch.
   c) Kate paid for her lunch.

3. **a)** Angela gets the most junk mail.
   b) Tina gets the most junk mail.
   c) Timothy gets the most junk mail.

4. **a)** Allan should be very careful.
   b) Allan should throw the offer away.
   c) Allan should consider the offer.

5. **a)** I can always get really good deals there.
   b) That store is open seven days a week.
   c) I don't like to go to that store.

6. **a)** Senator Gleason is giving a testimonial.
   b) Senator Gleason is on a bandwagon.
   c) Senator Gleason is using name-calling.

7. **a)** I was insulting.
   b) The telemarketer was insulting.
   c) The supervisor was insulting.

8. **a)** The boss might fire Eric.
   b) Eric needs a better paying job.
   c) The boss might give Eric a raise.

9. **a)** The telemarketer wasn't interested.
   b) I wasn't interesting.
   c) The telemarketer wasn't interesting.

10. **a)** She was probably using critical thinking.
    b) She must have been famished.
    c) She might have been card stacking.

EXERCISE 3

Directions: *Listen to the conversation. Each time you hear the bell, circle the sentence that you think is correct.*

1. **a)** The man is calling to sell something.
   b) The man isn't calling to sell something.

2. **a)** The man is calling to sell something.
   b) The man isn't calling to sell something.

3. **a)** The man is calling to sell something.
   b) The man isn't calling to sell something.

4. **a)** The man is interested in the program.
   b) The man is not interested in the program.

5. **a)** The man is interested in the program.
   b) The man is not interested in the program.

EXERCISE 4

Directions: You will hear three selections. At the beginning of each conversation you will hear a question. Listen to the conversation. Then, circle the best answer.

1. **a)** stacking the cards (fear)
   b) a tacky testimonial
   c) the old bait and switch

2. **a)** an exercise program
   b) walking shoes
   c) orange juice

3. **a)** stacking the cards (fear)
   b) bandwagon
   c) name-calling

EXERCISE 5

Directions: Listen to the sentence. Choose the correct vocabulary word.

1. **a)** telemarketer
   b) scam
   c) bandwagon

2. **a)** telemarketer
   b) complimentary
   c) junk mail

3. **a)** disruptive
   b) plain folks
   c) boss

4. **a)** ingenious
   b) persuasion
   c) unlimited

5. **a)** transfer
   b) testimonial
   c) name-calling

6. **a)** persuasion
   b) bait and switch
   c) name-calling

7. **a)** I think it's intelligent.
   b) I think it's dishonest.
   c) I think it's confusing.

8. **a)** glittering generalities
   b) card stacking (fear)
   c) buyer beware

9. **a)** solicitor
   b) consumer
   c) disruptive

10. **a)** critical thinking
    b) persuasion
    c) propaganda

PART SIX

USING IT: PRODUCT DESIGN AND ADVERTISING

For this exercise, you will create a product, and then write an advertisement for it.

Directions:

After your instructor has placed you into groups, decide the following:

1. What type of product is it? Is it a food item, a household goods item, an appliance, a car, or something else? What is the name of your product?

2. What is the design of your product? How big is it, how much does it weigh, what does it look like? How will the product be used? What is the target audience for this product (children, adults, teenagers, seniors, only men, only women)?

3. How will you advertise the product? Will you have a TV or radio commercial, a newspaper ad, or some other form of advertisement?

4. What kind of attractive visual aids (posters, pictures, maps or charts) and/or effective sound effects (music, street noise, or other appropriate sounds) will you use in your ad to ensure that it catches the target audience's attention?

After your group has decided on the design and type of advertisement for your product, create the ad. Be sure to include at least one propaganda device in the ad. Be creative! Remember, your goal is to get as many people as possible to buy your product so your company can make money.

Present your ads to the class. After each presentation, the class can guess which propaganda device each group used. Then, take a class vote to decide which ad was the favorite.

How Green Are You?

PART ONE

PRE-LISTENING: ENERGY EFFICIENCY SURVEY

environment
The air, water, and land that humans, animals, and plants share
Green movement
Organizations where people are active in environmental issues
conservation
To protect something from being lost or wasted; to save something
fossil fuels
Fuels that are formed in the ground from the remains of dead plants and animals that lived millions of years ago
efficient
Doing something well without wasting money, time, or energy

Protecting the **environment** is an important concern for people throughout the world. A major focus of the **Green movement** is energy **conservation**. Modern life depends on **fossil fuels** to make energy. The burning of coal, oil, and natural gas creates the energy we need to grow food, heat and cool our homes, make electricity and gasoline, and create many of the products we find on our store shelves. Because fossil fuels are in limited supply, it's important that we are as energy **efficient** as possible in our daily lives.

EXERCISE 1

Using What You Already Know
Directions: Take a look at the following survey to find out how energy efficient your lifestyle is. For each section, read the question and circle the answer. Then, write your total score for that section.

Energy Efficiency Survey

Do you make energy efficient choices at home? Answer these questions to find out.	Always	Sometimes	Never
1. Do you leave your heater on all night?	1	2	3
2. Do you take showers that are longer than five minutes?	1	2	3
3. Do you turn your computer, TV, radio, and other equipment off when you're done using them?	3	2	1
4. Do you wash your clothes in warm or cold water, instead of hot water?	3	2	1
5. Do you leave the water running while brushing your teeth?	1	2	3
6. Do you turn off the lights when you leave a room?	3	2	1
Total score for this section:			

rechargeable
Batteries that can be used again after putting a new supply of electricity into them

recycle
Reusing materials instead of throwing them away

Do you make energy efficient choices in the store and other places? Answer these questions to find out.	Always	Sometimes	Never
1. Do you use **rechargeable** batteries in your portable electronic devices?	3	2	1
2. Do you **recycle** newspapers, glass, aluminum, or plastic?	3	2	1
3. Do you use public transportation?	3	2	1
4. Do you buy products made from recycled materials?	3	2	1
5. Do you buy products that have little packaging and wrapping?	3	2	1
6. Do you ask that groceries and other things you buy be put in paper bags instead of plastic?	3	2	1
Total score for this section:			

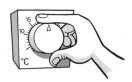

appliances
Large machines, such as refrigerators, stoves, dishwashers, and washing machines

double-pane
Windows that have two sheets of glass to save energy

compact fluorescent
Lights that use a lot less energy than regular light bulbs

thermostat
An instrument that controls the temperature of a heater

programmable
Something that you can set to turn on and off at specific times

low-flow
A special shower head that uses less water

Is your home energy efficient? Answer these questions to find out.	Yes	No
1. Are the **appliances** in your home energy efficient?	2	1
2. Are the windows in your home **double-pane**?	2	1
3. Have you replaced some of the regular incandescent light bulbs in your home with **compact fluorescent** light bulbs?	2	1
4. Is your hot water heater **thermostat** set at 120 degrees (or *low*)?	2	1
5. Do you have a **programmable** thermostat for your heater?	2	1
6. Do you have a **low-flow** shower head?	2	1
Total score for this section:		

Survey Results

How energy efficient are you? Add your total score for the three sections and check your results.

If your total score is:

40–48: Very good! You are being very energy efficient.

29–39: Good start, but there's more you need to do.

18–28: Oh no! You need to make some big changes to be more efficient!

Compare your scores in groups. Who is the most energy efficient? If you are unhappy with your score, what will you do to change your lifestyle?

PART TWO

EXERCISE 1

MAIN DIALOGUE

Scanning for the Main Idea/Background Information

Directions: Listen to the dialogue and try to get a general idea of what is happening. Remember, you don't need to understand everything. Just try to think about the following questions:

1. What is the main idea of this dialogue?
2. Where do you think the dialogue is taking place?
3. What role does each speaker have?
4. What level of education do you think each speaker has?
5. How do you think each speaker sounds (warm, cold, concerned, angry, and so on)?

Scanning for the Important Points

Directions: Now, listen to the dialogue again to answer these questions:

1. What kind of show is *How Green Are You*?

2. What do they have to do to win the game?

3. What general environmental issue are the first three quiz questions about?

4. What general environmental issue are the rest of the quiz questions about?

5. Who wins the game? How?

6. What does the winner get? What is special about the prize?

Scanning for Specific Pieces of Information

Directions: Listen to the dialogue one more time. Then, fill in the chart with information about the quiz questions. Note that some of these questions give energy-saving tips while others simply provide facts.

Topic	Energy-Saving Tips	Environmental Facts
Question 1		
Question 2		
Question 3		
Question 4		
Question 5		
Question 6		
Question 7		

EXERCISE 4

Vocabulary in Context

Directions: Listen to these sentences from the dialogue and circle the answer that has the same meaning.

1. *a)* Try to win a game.
   b) Try to play a game.

2. *a)* Waste the water.
   b) Save the water.

3. *a)* You will notice a big change.
   b) You will notice a small change.

4. *a)* a model 247 refrigerator
   b) It's on all of the time.

5. *a)* Sally is ahead.
   b) Jim is ahead.

6. *a)* Your tires should be full.
   b) Your tires should have gas.

7. *a)* This information is surprising.
   b) This information is unusual.

8. *a)* The cups are made from material that's better for the environment.
   b) The cups are made from material that's bad for the environment.

9. *a)* They don't read the paper.
   b) They put the paper in the trash.

10. *a)* If I'm first, I will get the answer correct.
    b) If I'm first, I will win the money.

EXERCISE 5

Directions: In pairs or small groups, discuss the following questions. Then, as a class, compare your answers.

1. What new information about conservation did you learn from the game show *How Green Are You?*

2. Why do you think so many people do not recycle their newspapers, cans, and other materials? What can we do to get more people to participate in recycling?

3. If you had a choice between buying a cheap refrigerator that is not energy efficient or an expensive refrigerator that saves a lot of energy, which would you buy? Why?

4. Do you feel the price you pay for energy (gas, electricity, gasoline) is cheap or expensive? Why? Do you feel people should have to pay more money for electricity and gasoline to make sure that they conserve these fuels? Explain.

5. Are people's attitudes toward the environment in the United States similar to or different from those in your native country? Explain.

PART THREE

EXPANSION

EXERCISE 1

endangered species
An animal or plant that may soon not exist anymore

grass-roots campaign
A movement for change that starts with ordinary people rather than government officials or other leaders

Section 1 Earth Day and Environmental Problems
Directions: Read the following and discuss with your teacher.

Earth Day

Earth Day is a special day set aside each year to focus on how we humans interact with the environment around us. Earth Day is celebrated in a variety of ways. Special classroom lessons on important issues, including conservation and **endangered species** protection are presented. Other activities include tree-planting ceremonies, rallies and demonstrations, and beach cleaning and recycling campaigns. Earth Day began in the United States in 1970 as a **grass-roots campaign** by college students and local communities to focus attention on the importance of taking care of the planet, and it has grown into a worldwide event. On April 22, Earth Day reminds us that our water, air, and land are an essential part of life on this planet.

Now, in pairs or small groups, answer these questions.

1. Is Earth Day celebrated in your native country? If yes, describe how it is celebrated.

2. Have you ever participated in an Earth Day event? If yes, talk about how you participated.

3. Make a list of as many specific environmental problems as you can think of. For each problem, discuss what you think caused the problem and what we can do to solve it. When you have finished, share your list with the rest of the class. Then, as a class, figure out which five problems were the most commonly cited.

EXERCISE 2

Directions: *Listen to the following Earth Day speakers describe environmental problems. For each speaker, listen to find the problem, the causes, effects, and solutions. Take notes. Don't worry about spelling.*

	Environmental Problem	Causes	Effects
Speaker 1			
Speaker 2			
Speaker 3			

EXERCISE 1

Section 2 Environmental Organizations and Volunteerism

Directions: Listen to the following descriptions of groups and organizations working on environmental issues. Write the name and purpose of the organization in the chart.

Name of Organization	Purpose of Organization
1.	
2.	
3.	
4.	
5.	

EXERCISE 2

Directions: In pairs or small groups, discuss these questions. Then, compare your answers with the rest of the class.

1. How many of these organizations have you heard about? How did you find out about them?

2. How do you think these organizations get money to conduct their educational programs and other activities?

3. Most of the people who work for organizations like *Zero Population Growth* are *volunteers*--they do not get paid for their work. What are some of the reasons that people volunteer to do work?

4. If you were going to volunteer to work for an environmental organization, which one would it be? Why? What sort of work would you volunteer to do?

5. Besides environmental organizations, there are many other groups that do good work. What are some of those organizations? Which one would you want to volunteer to work for?

nonprofit
An organization that works to help people; it does not earn a profit and does not have to pay taxes

Oral Journal Homework Assignment

*Directions: For this speech, you will talk about a **nonprofit** organization that you would like to volunteer to work for. In selecting an organization, first think about one whose work you feel is important. (You may use any of the organizations from Section 2 in Part Three, or any other that you are familiar with.) Next, think about the kind of work that they do. What specifically would you do for that organization? Is this something that you can do now, or would you need to train for it? Make sure the work is something you would enjoy and be able to do. Once you have selected* *the organization, make sure to get enough information about the group and what your volunteer experience might be like. Share with the class.*

Use the following rough outline as a guide.

I.   Introduction
   A. Organization you've chosen
   B. Reason for choosing organization

II. Overview
   A. General facts
      1. historical background of organization
      2. locations of work
   B. Kinds of projects
      1.
      2.

III. What you would do
   A. Physical work
   B. Planning/organizing
   C. Counseling/teaching
   D. Persuading

IV. How experience would affect your life
   A.
   B.

V.   Conclusion
   A. Summary of volunteer choice
   B. Why others should think about volunteering for this organization or a similar one

PART FOUR

FOCUS: COMPOUND NOUN STRESS VERSUS NOUN PHRASE STRESS

You have already learned the difference between *compound nouns* and *noun phrases:*

A *noun phrase* is the combination of an adjective + a noun.

Examples: a recycled newspaper
               a healthy environment
               a rechargeable battery

When you hear a noun phrase, you know that the first word just tells you what kind of noun the second word is. It does not change the meaning of the noun.

A *compound noun* is a noun + noun or an adjective + noun that takes on a new meaning from the original noun. Compound nouns can be two words combined into one, or two separate words. Compound nouns have new meanings from the main (second) noun.

Examples: a tiebreaker
               an air conditioner

Notice that *tiebreaker* and *air conditioner* have very different meanings from their main nouns *breaker* and *conditioner.*

When compound nouns are the result of an adjective + a noun, they can easily be mistaken for noun phrases that use the same words but have very different meanings.

For example:

Noun phrase: After a lot of careful thought, he chose the red *cross.*
                          (He chose a cross that was red.)

Compound noun: After a lot of careful thought, he chose the Red Cross.
                          (He chose to volunteer to work for the Red Cross organization.)

Good listeners can tell the difference in meaning between these two sentences because of their differing stress patterns.

With the noun phrase, the stress is on the noun, *cross* (the second word). It has the normal meaning. The speaker is talking about a *cross.*

With the compound noun, the stress is on the adjective, *red* (the first word).

Example: After a lot of careful thought, he chose the **Red** Cross.

Said this way, the sentence has a new meaning. The speaker is talking about an *organization* and not a *cross.*

Knowing how the stress of identical word combinations differ will help you to become a better listener.

EXERCISE 1

Directions: Listen to the following sentences. Choose the correct answer according to where you hear the stress.

Example: *a)* dirty *work*
                     b) *dirty* work

The correct answer is *a* because the stress in on the second word in the phrase.

1. *a)* *wild* life
    b) wild*life*

2. *a)* *green*house
    b) green *house*

3. *a)* a *dark*room
    b) a dark *room*

4. *a)* *light*bulbs
    b) light *bulbs*

5. *a)* *black*birds
    b) black *birds*

6. *a)* *wet*suit
    b) wet *suit*

7. **a)** *early* bird
    b) early *bird*

8. **a)** *White* House
    b) white *house*

9. **a)** *super*market
    b) super *market*

10. **a)** *hot*plate
    b) hot *plate*

Directions: *Listen to the sentences again. Choose the correct sentence according to the meaning.*

Example:
    (**a)**) She has a belt that is black in color.
    b) She is an expert in martial arts.

The answer is *a.* The stress is on the second word. The phrase is a normal noun phrase and does not have a special meaning. The speaker is talking about a belt that is black.

    Letter *b* would have the stress on the first word. It would have the new meaning of a marital arts expert.

1. **a)** fish, birds, and other animals
    b) exciting, uncontrolled, or unusual lifestyle

2. **a)** a special building to grow plants and flowers
    b) a house that is green

3. **a)** a room that is dark
    b) a special room to develop photos

4. **a)** special bulbs that do not weigh a lot
    b) special bulbs that use less electricity

5. **a)** I'm talking about one special kind of bird.
    b) I'm talking about different birds that are black.

6. **a)** He was wearing a jacket, tie, and pants that were wet.
    b) He was wearing a special suit to go into the water.

7. **a)** a person who likes to get up early
    b) a bird that flies north, early in the spring

8. **a)** The man I am talking about is The President of the United States.
    b) The man I am talking about is someone who lives in a white house.

9. **a)** The market is really wonderful.
    b) It is a special kind of store that is very big and has all kinds of products.

10. **a)** a special appliance to cook things
    b) a plate that is very hot

PART FIVE

PRACTICE

Directions: *You will hear ten questions. Read the three possible responses and choose the correct answer.*

1. **a)** We are doing more to protect endangered species.
   b) I'm worried about my grades.
   c) The population keeps increasing.

2. **a)** Burn them.
   b) Recycle them.
   c) Throw them away.

3. **a)** Use compact fluorescent lightbulbs.
   b) Buy an SUV or other large car.
   c) Ask for plastic in the supermarket.

4. **a)** It's best at 120° F or low.
   b) Turn the water off when you are soaping up.
   c) Take showers instead of baths.

5. **a)** I just moved here.
   b) I always recycle.
   c) I have lots of energy.

6. **a)** It was a grass-roots campaign.
   b) on April 22, 1970
   c) to get the public attention focused on the environment

7. **a)** *Zero Population Growth* is a nonprofit organization.
   b) We need to reduce the number of people on the planet.
   c) You might try looking online.

8. **a)** When you buy food, you should always ask for paper bags.
   b) Recycling is an excellent way to reduce air and water pollution.
   c) The newspapers and cans are okay, but the plastic containers are not.

9. **a)** We must clean up the dirty lakes and rivers.
   b) We are not doing enough to stop it.
   c) We need to protect our marine wildlife.

10. **a)** Take the bus or other forms of public transportation.
    b) Get a programmable thermostat for your heater.
    c) Make sure you recycle all your glass, cans, and newspapers.

Directions: *You will hear ten sentences. Read the three choices and circle the correct answer.*

1. **a)** We need to recycle more.
   b) We need to drive less.
   c) We need to reduce air pollution.

2. **a)** Joe's wife didn't like the old refrigerator.
   b) Joe wants to lower his electric bill.
   c) Joe and his wife like to buy appliances.

3. *a)* We need to use less paper.
   b) We need to plant more trees.
   c) We need to pass laws to protect rain forests.

4. *a)* It takes a lot of time and money to run the organization.
   b) Your tax dollars support the organization.
   c) The organization needs public support.

5. *a)* If you replace the bulbs, your bill will be fifty dollars cheaper.
   b) You only have to replace some of your bulbs to save energy.
   c) Compact fluorescent bulbs use one quarter of the energy of regular bulbs.

6. *a)* an overweight animal
   b) a rich, powerful person
   c) a tiger

7. *a)* The pet is very warm.
   b) The food looks great.
   c) The person is very hardworking.

8. *a)* a painted board
   b) a metal board
   c) a chalk board

9. *a)* We are working hard to preserve fossil fuels.
   b) We are working hard to preserve the forests.
   c) We are working hard to preserve all of the environment.

10. *a)* The law began three years ago.
    b) The law will continue for three more years.
    c) The law is going to begin three years from now.

EXERCISE 3

Directions: Listen to the conversation. Each time you hear the bell, circle the sentence that you think is correct.

1. *a)* Mark has been hired for a new job.
   b) Mark has not been hired for a new job.

2. *a)* Mark has been hired for a new job.
   b) Mark has not been hired for a new job.

3. *a)* Mark is probably volunteering to do physical labor.
   b) Mark is probably volunteering to do nonphysical labor.

4. *a)* Mark is probably volunteering to do physical labor.
   b) Mark is probably volunteering to do nonphysical labor.

5. *a)* Mark is volunteering for this organization because he likes the work.
   b) Mark is volunteering for this organization because he likes the other volunteers.

6. *a)* Mark is volunteering for this organization because he likes the work.
   b) Mark is volunteering for this organization because he likes the other volunteers.

EXERCISE 4

Directions: *You will hear two passages. At the beginning of each passage, you will hear a question. Listen to the passage. Then, circle the best answer.*

1. a) toxic household products
   b) business and industry
   c) increasing health problems

2. a) at an Audubon Society meeting
   b) at a Zero Population Growth activity
   c) at an Earth Day rally

EXERCISE 5

Directions: *Listen to the sentence. Choose the correct vocabulary word.*

1. a) car
   b) sofa
   c) dishwasher

2. a) conservation
   b) greenhouse
   c) grass-roots

3. a) endangered species
   b) competed
   c) dumped

4. a) wildlife
   b) mind-boggling
   c) conservation

5. a) green movement
   b) environment
   c) wildlife

6. a) volunteer
   b) programmable
   c) efficient

7. a) loot
   b) dump
   c) fossil fuel

8. a) inflate
   b) recycle
   c) double-pane

9. a) inflated
   b) zip
   c) 24/7

10. a) programmable
    b) low-flow
    c) fluorescent

PART SIX

USING IT: TAKING THE GREEN PLEDGE

In this chapter, we have discussed many environmental problems. To make the world a greener, healthier planet, our governments and large business corporations must make serious changes. But, conservation is also a personal decision. There are specific actions that individuals can take in their everyday lives that will help conserve our beautiful land, air, and water. For this exercise, you will take a Green Pledge. You will make a list of actions and then promise to carry them out for one week to see how easy it is to contribute to a healthier planet.

Directions: *Follow these steps.*

Step One: Write your Green Pledge

Decide as a class what activities to include. Will you promise not to drive for an entire week? Take shorter showers for a week? Recycle newspapers, bottles, and cans for one week? You can make your list long or short. Make sure that your list includes activities that everyone can participate in. Also, decide when your week will begin and end. When your list is complete, have everyone sign the pledge and promise to do the activities.

Step Two: Your Green Week

During your Green week, keep a journal of your activities and feelings. Write down what you do (for example, how many items you recycle, or how long your showers are) and your reaction to these changes. Is being Green inconvenient or easy? Write down all your ideas.

Step Three: Share Your Results

After your Green week is over, bring your journals to class and discuss your experiences and reactions. In small groups, discuss these questions:

1. In general, how did you feel about this experience?
2. Did your friends and family know what you were doing? If yes, what did they think about your pledge?
3. What was the most difficult thing that you had to do? Explain.
4. What was the easiest thing that you had to do? Explain.
5. Which of the things do you plan to continue to do? Why?
6. Which of the things do you think you will not continue to do? Why not?
7. Has this experience changed the way you feel about the environment? Explain.
8. What other kinds of changes do you plan to make to help the environment?

Step Four: Class Results

As a class, compile statistics that show how well the class was able to carry out their pledges.

First, prepare a chart that shows all of the actions that you pledged to carry out. Next, tally the number of students who were able to honor the pledge for each action. Using these numbers, prepare graphs that clearly represent the results. Finally, analyze the results. Can you think of reasons why the class did better in some areas than in others? Can you think of ways to improve in the areas that were difficult? How did the class as a whole benefit from this project?